PASSING ON THE
MANTLE

The Elijah Legacy

MORRIS CERULLO
WITH PATRICIA HULSEY

First Edition – 2006

MORRIS CERULLO WORLD EVANGELISM
U.S.: P.O. Box 85277 • San Diego, CA 92186 • (858) 277-2200
U.K.: P.O. Box 277 • Hemel Hempstead HERTS HP2 7DH • (01442) 232-432
CANADA: P.O. Box 3600 • Concord, Ontario L4K 1B6 • (905) 669-1788
www.mcwe.com   E-mail: morriscerullo@mcwe.com

TABLE OF CONTENTS

INTRODUCTION

THE FATHER'S MANTLE

PART ONE

ELIJAH

PART TWO

PASSING ON THE MANTLE

PART THREE

ELISHA

APPENDICES

THE FATHER'S MANTLE

INTRODUCTION

He bursts on the scene with little introduction, but with a burning passion and a God-given call which impacted the destiny of entire nations. The Bible identifies him as Elijah, the Tishbite, and he is forever associated with powerful proclamations, supernatural provision, resurrection of the dead, fire from heaven, power in prayer, and the double-portion anointing of a young man named Elisha.

In the Church today, we have sung about the *"Days of Elijah,"* we have talked about the double-portion anointing, and we have coined phrases such as the "Elijah generation." But if we are to really experience the double-portion anointing that God has reserved for us and pass it on to others, we must have a revelation of this Prophet Elijah and his young protegee, Elisha.

Through the pages of this book, we will take a spiritual journey back through time. We will first follow in the footsteps of Elijah as he stands boldly before Ahab and declares God's judgment. We will sit with him at the Brook Cherith and accompany him to the widow's house. We will witness the supernatural provision of God in a time of famine and the raising of the dead. We will stand with him on Mount Carmel as the fire falls from Heaven, we will travail with him in prayer, and we will experience his anguish as he flees for his life.

Later, we will accompany Elijah by the field where he casts his mantle over a young chosen vessel called Elisha. We will then walk together with them as Elisha is prepared to receive the mantle of his beloved mentor. We will stand gazing upward as Elijah is taken and then we will journey on with Elisha as he puts into practice what he has learned from Elijah and begins to exercise the double-portion anointing.

A SPIRITUAL PATTERN

As we take this journey together, we will weave together a spiritual pattern for the supernatural mantle that must rest upon our own lives if we are to receive the mantle and experience of the unique, double-portion anointing to impact our world as did these two men.

When we speak of the mantle of Elijah, we are not talking about some sacred shroud or religious antiquity. The mantle that descended upon Elisha represents God's sacred call, the destiny, and the anointing that rested upon Elijah.

The shroud that was passed on to Elisha was aged and worn. It had served Elijah well. It was with him during the cold lonely nights in the wilderness. He had used it to wrap himself when he prayed. The mantle was with Elijah on Mt. Carmel as he confronted a wicked king and backslidden Israel and called down fire from heaven.

On the mount of God when he heard the still small voice of God calling him, Elijah wrapped his face in the mantle and stood outside the cave to commune with Him. Later, at God's direction, he cast the mantle upon Elisha as he was out in the field plowing, signifying God's spiritual mandate to Elisha.

For years Elisha shadowed Elijah. They ate together. They traveled together. They prayed together. Elisha witnessed the mighty manifestation of God's power as Elijah ministered in supernatural power and authority.

Years later, when he and Elisha stood at the Jordan River, Elijah twisted the mantle in his hands and smote the river. The waters parted, and they walked together across the river on dry ground.

MY FATHER, MY FATHER

When the time came for Elijah to go to the Heavenly Father, he looked down upon Elisha from the fiery chariot and, in that final fleeting moment, the mantle fell from his shoulders and landed at Elisha's feet. Elisha, with one final glimpse of his mentor and a heartfelt cry, "My father, My father–the chariots and horsemen of Israel," was parted from his beloved father in the faith.

"My father, my father!" A heart-rending cry. Two words. Simple words, yet vital to the understanding of the strategy for passing on the double-portion anointing.

These two words reveal that this supernatural mantle that will impact future generations cannot be passed on through teaching alone. It can only be passed on through an impartation of supernatural life. It must be imparted through a divine spiritual connection that emulates the father and son relationship.

There is a difference between a teacher and a father. A teacher imparts information. A father imparts life and implants destiny. You can impart information to someone and they can still miss their destiny. A father invests his life in his children. It is not a 9 to 5 job. He keeps his children on course with destiny.

Elijah had developed a spiritual father/son relationship with Elisha. This type of intimacy was prophesied by Malachi when he declared:

Behold, I will send you Elijah the prophet before the coming of the great and dreadful day of the Lord. And he shall turn the heart of the fathers to the children, and the heart of the children to their fathers...

Malachi 4:5-6

A vital part of the Elijah anointing is to turn the hearts of children to the fathers—not only in the natural world, but in the spiritual world. The hearts of spiritual fathers must be bonded to their spiritual children, and the hearts of spiritual children to their fathers.

GOD YOUR FATHER

For those who had a good father in the natural world, this spiritual concept of fatherhood will be easily grasped. For others who experienced an abusive or absentee father, it may be more difficult. But we must base our concept of spiritual fatherhood on God's Word, not on the basis of what we have experienced in the natural world.

This concept of spiritual fatherhood goes back to the Garden of Eden. In the beginning, God the Father created a son and a daughter—Adam and Eve—and commissioned them to multiply naturally through childbirth and spiritually by reproducing a generation that would relate to Him as they did: As sons and daughters to their Father.

God breathed into Adam and Eve the breath of His own life. He gave them a spiritual commission and a divine destiny. He fostered intimate relationship with them to equip them for the task. Tragically, Genesis 3 records the sad account of their failure and the subsequent judgments brought upon this world through their sin.

Adam should have learned from God the Father to be a spiritual father who would reveal God's heart to the rest of the world. This first couple should have reproduced spiritual children and passed on the intimate relationship they had with their Heavenly Father.

THE FATHER OF NATIONS

This mandate of spiritual fatherhood was passed on to Abraham when he was chosen by God to be the father of nations. God declared: *As for me, this is my covenant with you: You will be the father of many nations. No longer will you be called Abram; your name will be Abraham, for I have made you a father of many nations* (Genesis 17:4-5).

As a spiritual father of nations, through Abraham all the nations of the earth were to be blessed: *"And in thy seed shall all the nations of the earth be blessed"* (Genesis 22:18).

The New Testament reveals that as believers, we are heirs to the same promises God gave Abraham:

> *Know ye therefore that they which are of faith, the same are the children of Abraham. And the Scripture, foreseeing that God would justify the heathen through faith, preached before the Gospel unto Abraham saying, In thee shall all nations be blessed. So then they which be of faith are blessed with faithful Abraham.*

> Galatians 3:7-9

You are an heir of the promises of Abraham because you are the seed of Abraham through salvation in Jesus Christ, *"And if ye be Christ's, then are ye Abraham's seed, and heirs according to the promises"* (Galatians 3:29).

As the seed of Abraham, you are an heir of the promise of salvation, but you are also heir to much more. You are under commission to bless the nations of the world with the good news of the Gospel. You are under divine commission to be a spiritual father, as was Abraham. This commission to spiritual fatherhood is for both men and women alike.

WHAT MAKES A FATHER?

A person doesn't become a parent simply because he produces a child. A person must have the heart of a father and function as a father. So, what are the qualities of a spiritual father? As a spiritual father whose life was to impact the nations, Abraham is an excellent model to study. The following spiritual qualities were evidenced in his life:

He was strong in faith: Abraham is perhaps best known for what was accounted to him as faith. He had such faith that he praised God for the fulfillment of God's promises before they were manifested: *"He [Abraham] staggered not at the promise of God through unbelief, but was strong in faith, giving glory to God"* (Romans 4:20).

Abraham was completely sure God was able to do anything He promised (Romans 4:20). Abraham was fully persuaded that God would bless the nations of the world through him, *"And being fully persuaded, that, what He had promised, He was able also to perform"* (Romans 4:21).

The magnitude of the vision to which God has called you is overwhelming, but do not stagger at His promises. Do not look to the greatness of the task before you, but look to the greatness of your God. Be like Abraham who *"... believed God even though such as promise just couldn't come to pass"* (Romans 4:18, The Living Bible).

He invested in spiritual things: Abraham invested his whole life in that which was not visible in the natural world. God gave Abraham the promise of a beautiful land, yet he himself never set foot in this country:

And He gave him none inheritance in it, no not so much as to set his foot on: Yet He promised that He would give it to him for a possession, and to his seed after him, when as yet he had no child.

Acts 7:5

A land was promised which Abraham had not seen, promised to a son he did not have. Yet Abraham did not doubt God. He invested his life in the plan of God for the benefit of future generations.

Although he had no son, Abraham received the promise to be the father of many nations. In the natural it looked hopeless. But in the face of hopelessness, Abraham *"...against hope believed in hope, that he might become the father of many nations according to that which was spoken, So shall thy seed be"* (Romans 4:18).

No matter what your circumstances, no matter how hopeless your situation, know that the vision God has called you to will be fulfilled. Face hopelessness with assurance that *"what He has promised, He is able also to perform"* (Romans 4:21).

As an Elijah raising up Elishas, you will spend your whole life invested in that which is not visible, but the results are eternal. Generations to come will be blessed because you fulfill the mandate.

Abraham also invested his resources in spiritual things. He paid tithes of all he owned (Genesis 14:20).

Your commission as part of The Elijah Institute will involve wise use of your financial resources. Are you willing to invest all for the sake of the call?

He was obedient to the call of God: When Abraham was called by God to go out to a place which he would later receive for an inheritance, he obeyed:

> *By faith, Abraham, when he was called to go out into a place which he should after receive for an inheritance, obeyed; and he went out, not knowing whither he went.*

Hebrews 11:8

It is not enough to be called to the vision of The Elijah Institute. You must respond in obedience to that calling.

He was willing to stand alone: God declares, *"Look unto Abraham you father, and unto Sarah that bare you: for I called him alone, and blessed him, and increased him"* (Isaiah 51:2).

Abraham was called alone. He had to leave his homeland and his family in answer to that call: *"Now the Lord had said unto Abram , Get thee out of thy country, and from thy kindred, and from thy father's house, unto a land that I will shew thee"* (Genesis 12:1).

God said of Abraham, *"Look unto Abraham your father, and unto Sarah that bare you: for I called him alone , and blessed him, and increased him"* (Isaiah 51:2).

Responding to the mandate of The Elijah Institute may involve leaving home and family. Certainly it will involve stepping out from among unconcerned believers who have not yet caught this vision. You may have to stand alone. Are you willing?

> *And every one that hath forsaken houses, or brethren, or sisters, or father, or mother, or wife, or children, or lands, for my name's sake, shall receive an hundredfold, and shall inherit everlasting life.*

Matthew 19:29

He had spiritual vision: Abraham's vision was of a city whose builder was God, *"For he looked for a city which hath foundations, whose builder and maker is God"* (Hebrews 11:10).

His vision caused him to stay in a strange land, dwelling in tents, separated from his home and family. The vision changed his life and his lifestyle.

The vision of The Elijah Institute will change your life. You will never again be the same. You cannot be content with the temporal things of life because you seek a higher, eternal cause.

He knew God intimately: Abraham was called, "the friend of God":

> *And the Scripture was fulfilled which saith, Abraham believed God, and it was imputed unto him for righteousness: and he was called the Friend of God.*

James 2:23

It will require intimate personal relationship with God in order for you to fulfill the vision of The Elijah Institute. You cannot foster a father/son relationship with Elishas if you do not have a Father/son relationship with God yourself. You must become a friend of God.

He was prompt to do God's will: When God spoke to Abraham that the sign of the covenant between him and God was to be circumcision, the Bible records that the same day God spoke, Abraham had all the men in his family circumcised (Genesis 17).

Some time later God fulfilled His promise to Abraham and he and his wife, Sarah, had a son. After the birth of Isaac, God gave Abraham a difficult test. He told him to sacrifice his son (Genesis 22).

In Isaac was the future of the promises of God. He was the heir through whom Abraham's descendants were to come. Isaac was to bring forth the nation of Israel through which the world was to be blessed. Yet God asked Abraham to sacrifice his son.

The Bible records in Genesis 22:3 that after Abraham received this message from God, he rose up early in the morning to obey the instructions. Even when God's will was difficult, Abraham did not delay. When God spoke he acted immediately and, because of his obedience, God provided another sacrifice and Isaac's life was spared.

When you step forward in obedience God will always move in your behalf.

It is interesting to note that Abraham never referred to God's instructions regarding Isaac as a sacrifice. He called it worship. The highest form of worship is to look beyond Isaac–beyond the ministry, beyond that which we love–to God.

God has given you a divine mandate that has changed your life, but never can this ministry and its mantle become more important than God. God tested Abraham to see if it was Isaac who occupied his highest devotion or God. It must always be God who occupies your highest allegiance. The vision can never replace the Giver of the vision.

He was mobile for God: Abraham lived a life which enabled complete mobility for God. He could move quickly at God's command (Genesis 12). Stay unencumbered. Don't become too settled.

He walked in revelation knowledge: Abraham acted upon revelation from God instead of human reasoning. God frequently shared supernatural revelation with him, declaring *"Shall I hide from Abraham that thing which I do?"* (Genesis 18:17). Learn to walk in revelation knowledge. Don't be led by your emotions or your own natural reasoning.

He did not look to his own abilities: God's promise to the nations sprang from one as good as dead because, in the natural, Abraham had no ability to fulfill God's plan: *"Therefore sprang there even of one, and him as good as dead, so many as the stars of the sky in multitude, and as the sand which is by the sea shore innumerable"* (Hebrews 11:12).

When the divine mandate from God was given to Abraham, his past had been unproductive and his present was still unproductive. But he did not accept the deadness of his own body and of Sarah's womb:

> *Therefore from one man, and him as good as dead, were born as many as the stars by the sky in multitude, innumerable as the sand which is by the seashore.*

> Hebrews 11:12

You may have felt dead and unproductive in the past, but all that is changing. Right now! Today! From you—one person, perhaps as good as dead—will be born multitudes!

THE FATHER AND HIS SON

Perhaps the greatest example of the spiritual father/son relationship is in that modeled by Jesus during His earthly ministry. Even as a child, Jesus embraced His relationship with the Father, declaring that He must be about His Father's business (Luke 2:49). At the time of Christ's baptism, the Father confirmed the intimacy of this relationship, declaring *"this is my beloved Son, in whom I am well pleased"* (Matthew 3:17).

Throughout His entire ministry, Jesus did nothing but what pleased the Father. The words He spoke were from the Father. The works He did were the Father's works. To see Jesus was to see the Father:

> *If ye had known me, ye should have known my Father also: and from henceforth ye know him, and have seen him. Philip saith unto him, Lord, shew us the Father, and it sufficeth us. Jesus saith unto him, Have I been so long time with you, and yet hast thou not known me, Philip? he that hath seen me hath seen the Father; and how sayest thou then, Shew us the Father? Believest thou not that I am in the Father, and the Father in me? the words that I speak unto you I speak not of myself: but the Father that dwelleth in me, he doeth the works. Believe me that I am in the Father, and the Father in me: or else believe me for the very works' sake.*

John 4:7-11

Towards the end of His ministry, Jesus declared, *"Verily, verily, I say unto you, He that believeth on me, the works that I do shall he do also; and greater works than these shall he do; because I go unto my Father"* (John 4:12).

The spiritual children of Jesus–the disciples–would do greater works because Jesus was going to be with the Father. Likewise, the generation of Elishas that you raise up will continue the greater works when you go to be with the Father.

Spiritual multiplication comes from producing life. Jesus sowed life. He taught the words of life and did the works of life. Jesus poured life into His 12 disciples. From these 12 came the 70. From the 70 came the 120 in the upper room. From the 120 came a multitude when God added 3,000 to the church in one day...and the process continues down to this day.

THE APOSTLES WERE SPIRITUAL FATHERS

The New Testament books of the Acts and the Epistles reveal that the Apostles embraced this concept of spiritual fatherhood. The Apostle Paul declared, *"For though ye have ten thousand instructors in Christ, yet have ye not many fathers : for in Christ Jesus I have begotten you through the gospel"* (1 Corinthians 4:15).

There are many who teach, preach, and evangelize–but where are those who will birth and nurture spiritual sons and daughters? That is the fundamental strategy which we in The Elijah Institute must grasp. Passing on the mantle takes more than just teaching. It is a spiritual birth and nurturing process.

As a spiritual father, Paul modeled the anointing for his sons and daughters. He declared, *"Wherefore I beseech you, be ye followers of me"* (1 Corinthians 4:16). To declare something like this, you must be walking worthy before the Lord. You must know your own destiny and know where you are going spiritually. Spiritual fathers cannot be immature, fleshly, emotion-led men.

This does not mean that, as a spiritual model, Paul hid his struggles from his spiritual sons and daughters. He clearly explained his problems and challenges:

> *For we would not, brethren, have you ignorant of our trouble which came to us in Asia, that we were pressed out of measure, above strength, insomuch that we despaired even of life: But we had the sentence of death in ourselves, that we should not trust in ourselves, but in God which raiseth the dead: Who delivered us from so great a death , and doth deliver: in whom we trust that he will yet deliver us; Ye also helping together by prayer for us, that for the gift bestowed upon us by the means of many persons thanks may be given by many on our behalf.*

2 Corinthians 1:8-11

As spiritual fathers, we cannot adequately prepare Elishas without revealing to them the inherent problems associated with cutting-edge ministry. We must be transparent. We must be real. We must let them know that there are great challenges, but our God is greater!

Repeatedly in his letters, Paul references this father/son relationship:

> *As ye know how we exhorted and comforted and charged every one of you, as a father doth his children, That ye would walk worthy of God, who hath called you unto his kingdom and glory.*

1 Thessalonians 2:1-12

> *My little children, of whom I travail in birth again until Christ be formed in you.* Galatians 4:19

Travail. Birth. Nurturing. Modeling. Commissioning to destiny. All vital functions of a spiritual father.

SEEKING A FATHER

In the natural world, this generation has sometimes been referred to as the fatherless generation. Absentee and abusive fathers, dysfunctional dads, and emotionally distant parents abound. Truly, this is a generation seeking a father.

I have always taught that all truth is parallel, meaning that we must look at the natural world to discern what is going on in the spiritual world. Just as there is a generation in the natural world crying out for a father, there is also a whole generation seeking spiritual fathers who will nurture them in the faith, commission them with the authority of God, and prepare them to fulfill their divine destinies. They have not found–nor will they find–what they are seeking in teachers who are emotionally distant and who disseminate information instead of revelation. Teachers abound. Spiritual fathers are scarce.

As you go forth under the Elijah anointing, don't strive to build your own Kingdom. Build sons and daughters instead. Let the anointing you have received from God flow through you to them. You cannot give what you have not received. You cannot educate life into another. You cannot command it or legislate it. You must impart it as it flows from God through you to them.

If you expect your spiritual children to succeed, then you must invest your life in them. As Elijah did Elisha. As Christ did with His disciples. As Paul did with Timothy and others. You must develop relationship. You must be a spiritual parent to them. You must learn to look beyond their generation to see the multitudes of generations that will be impacted as your spiritual children rise up to seize the mantle of God's anointing.

WE MUST TRANSFER OUR PASSION TO THE NEXT GENERATION

Our spiritual passion must be transferred to the next generation. The psalmist David declared that we must show

> *...to the generation to come the praises of the Lord, and his strength, and his wonderful works that he hath done... That the generation to come might know them, even the children which should be born; who should arise and declare them to their children: That they might set their hope in God, and not forget the works of God, but keep his commandments.*

Psalm 78:4-7

You will declare to the generation to come the works of God and that generation will pass it on to their spiritual children. As a spiritual Elijah, you will raise up sons and daughters from around the world.

Receive God's prophetic word to you today:

> Lift up thine eyes round about, and see: all they gather themselves together, they come to thee: thy sons shall come from far, and thy daughters shall be nursed at thy side. Then thou shalt see, and flow together, and thine heart shall fear, and be enlarged; because the abundance of the sea shall be converted unto thee, the forces of the Gentiles shall come unto thee.
>
> Isaiah 6:4-6

Your spiritual sons and daughters will come from afar. You will nurture them at your side. You will flow together in ministry and you will be literally overwhelmed at the magnitude of this vision. Your heart will be enlarged and the nations (Gentiles) will come to you!

You may have been spiritually barren in times past, but no more. God declares to you today:

> Sing, O barren, thou that didst not bear; break forth into singing, and cry aloud, thou that didst not travail with child: for more are the children of the desolate than the children of the married wife, saith the Lord. Enlarge the place of thy tent, and let them stretch forth the curtains of thine habitations: spare not, lengthen thy cords, and strengthen thy stakes; For thou shalt break forth on the right hand and on the left; and thy seed shall inherit the Gentiles, and make the desolate cities to be inhabited.
>
> Isaiah 54:1-4

Get ready. Put aside all small thinking. Enlarge your habitation. God has declared it: You are going to have a very large spiritual family!

TAKING UP THE MANTLE

As his spiritual father ascended to God, Elisha tore his clothes in anguish, ran to where Elijah's mantle had fallen on the ground, and picked it up. He held it in his hands, this symbol of the prophetic anointing of God's Spirit that had rested upon Elijah. When Elisha took up that mantle, it was symbolically infused with the same supernatural anointing that had rested upon it when it was in Elijah's possession.

Elisha wrapped the mantle together as he had seen Elijah do and walked to the banks of the Jordan River.

The mantle was only a symbol of God's anointing. Elisha knew that his title as Elijah's successor, his ministry, the mantle–everything–would be in vain unless the same power and anointing of God's Spirit that was upon Elijah rested upon him.

Elisha struck the mantle upon the waters and cried out, "Where is the Lord God of Elijah?" –and God responded in a demonstration of His power by parting the Jordan River just as He had done for Elijah. In the distance, fifty sons of the prophets who stood afar saw the demonstration of God's power and declared, "The spirit of Elijah rests on Elisha!"

From the day that mantle passed into his hands, Elisha went forth to minister in a double-portion anointing.

THE ELIJAH ANOINTING

The big question is, has the same power and anointing that rested upon Elijah and Elisha been delegated to us? The same miracle–working power that was manifested on behalf of Israel should be flowing within the Church today. Has the mantle of the anointing passed from the hands of Jesus into our hands when He ascended to His Father?

We ask, "Where is the Lord God of Elijah?"

God asks, "Where are the Elijahs of God?"

Are we ready to pick up the mantle of God's anointing and strike it upon the waters of our world?

- Are we ready to pick up the mantle of God's anointing and walk into the fulfillment of His promises and purposes?

- Are we ready to pick up the mantle of God's anointing and demonstrate the power of God by meeting the need of the world–healing the sick, proclaiming the Word, and bringing in an end-time harvest of souls?

- Are we ready to confront a world sick and dying in sin and come forth with an anointed word from the Lord–

to challenge the same worldly conditions Elijah challenged with a direct word from God?

WHAT DO YOU WANT OUT OF LIFE?

In 1969, during a crusade in Brazil, God asked me what I wanted out of life. I answered, "God, give me the ability to take what you have given me, the power and anointing that is upon my ministry and give it to others." Then God gave me a divine mandate: "Son, build Me an army."

Since that day, this commission has been the driving vision, passion, and purpose of my life and ministry. God has enabled us to train over 1.5 million people worldwide through our National Training Institutes and Schools of Ministry.

Just as the Prophet Elijah cast his mantle upon Elisha and a double portion anointing came upon him, God has enabled me to pass on the mantle of anointing on my life to spiritual sons and daughters of the Gospel who are now modern-day Elijahs. Hundreds of thousands of these Elijahs are right now in Africa, Central and South America, Mexico, Asia, Europe, India, the Middle East, and many other areas being used mightily by God to change the spiritual destinies of their nations.

Now, in the next level of intensification, we are establishing The Elijah Institute where these proven Elijahs will pass the mantle on to others–key leaders, successful pastors, evangelists, and teachers–with strong leadership abilities who are willing to take the special mentoring materials we have prepared and raise up Elishas, who then will be used to reach the lost and proclaim the Gospel in a demonstration of the power of God, with signs following. (For further information see Appendices Five, Six, and Seven).

That is why this book on *"Passing On The Mantle"* is so important. If The Elijah Institute is to fulfill its divine destiny, we must receive a new revelation of the double-portion anointing. We must learn how to receive this divine mantle from God and how to pass it on to the future generations, a new breed of men and women with a single purpose: Change the world!

God has revealed to me that it is time for Elijahs all over the world–those whose lives and destinies have been shaped by this ministry and others–to take up the mantle of God's anointing and train Elishas to carry on this vision.

LOOK AT YOUR HANDS

If you are familiar with this ministry, you know that I often tell you to

look at your hands, for in them lies the destinies of your nation and multitudes around the world. I ask you again, right now, to lay down this book for a moment and look at your hands. If you will reach out and accept the mantle of the double-portion that will be passed to you through the pages of this book, then you will go forth in the spirit and power of Elijah:

> *And he shall go before him in the spirit and power of Elias, to turn the hearts of the fathers to the children, and the disobedient to the wisdom of the just; to make ready a people prepared for the Lord.*

Luke 1:17

Your life will never again be the same as you function under the mantle of the new anointing God has for you. Your ministry will rise to a new level numerically as never before as you learn how to pass this mantle on to those around you, leaving a lasting legacy on the earth.

Look at your hands. Hear the voice of the Holy Spirit saying, "Where are the Elijahs of God?"

Ask God to open your mind to receive this revelation. Begin to embrace the vision right now in the spirit world. Visualize the mantle as it is descending upon you. Reach up and take hold of it. Receive the double-portion anointing as it is passed into your hands.

God's servant,

Morris Cerullo

CHAPTER ONE

THE DAYS OF ELIJAH

We sing "These are the days of Elijah," but what were the days of Elijah really like? If we are to understand the significance of the spiritual mantle that rested upon Elijah, then we must understand the context of the times in which he lived and ministered.

For over a hundred years, God's people prospered under the reigns of Saul, David, and Solomon. Although each of these men had sins and failures, generally speaking it was a glorious time for the kingdom. Towards the end of Solomon's reign, however, he allowed idolatry through foreign marriages, a practice which was forbidden by God (Deuteronomy 17:13-20 and Nehemiah 13:23-27). Solomon also levied excessive taxes and labor to satisfy his selfish extravagances.

When Rehoboam, Solomon's son, assumed the throne of his father, he refused the counsel of the older men to cut back on the oppressive taxation and actually threatened to increase taxes. As a result, 10 of the tribes seceded and the kingdom was divided. The northern kingdom was called Israel and the southern was referred to as Judah. This division continued for some 200 years until both kingdoms were eventually captured by foreign invaders.

During this time, the northern kingdom had 19 kings, all of whom were wicked. The southern kingdom had 17 rulers, eight of whom followed the Lord, nine of whom were wicked. During this period of the divided kingdom, God sent many prophets to warn his people, in both the northern and southern kingdoms.

An evil king named Ahab, who married a wicked woman named Jezebel, was ruler in the northern kingdom of Israel at the time Elijah entered the scene. Jezebel's father was Ethbaal, king of Zidonians and an idolatrous priest. Jezebel's religious heritage was idolatry, as she was a worshiper of Baal.

Baal was the chief god worshiped by the Canaanites. Baal is a Semitic word meaning "lord, master, or owner." The head of this pantheon of gods was called "El," and he was believed to be the father of some 70 gods. Baal was the most popular of these gods because he was considered the god of fertility in the human and animal realm, with power over the weather and the ability to perpetrate good crops. Each geographic area also worshiped its own Baal, frequently adding the name of the city or place where it was worshiped. For example, Baal-Hermon or Baal-Hazor.

Baalism included the worship of deities dedicated to sexual perversion, violence, and greed. It included the offering of incense, burnt sacrifices (sometimes human), and licentious sexual activity (Jeremiah 7:9; 19:5; 1 Kings 14:23-24; 15:12; 22:46).

The days of Elijah were actually a time of idolatry, murder, perversion, and deception. He was raised up in a time of conflict, political and moral decline, and spiritual apostasy.

THE SAME CONDITIONS EXIST TODAY

Does this sound like your nation today? In America, our nation began with a Godly heritage from which many have turned away. America is presently scarred by conditions similar to those that existed under Baalism: Greed, sex, violence, division, and idolatry. Flip through the television channels and you will see it on practically every station. Greed, sex, and violence are glorified in movies. People in America worship the idols of power, money, materialism, and entertainment. Our sports heroes and television stars are paid more than our teachers and law enforcement officers.

As in Baalism, America is even engaging in a form of child sacrifice as thousands of unborn babies are aborted annually. We kill them in the womb and in the birth canal and then burn their little broken bodies. Since the controversial legal decision in 1973 (Roe vs. Wade) which legalized abortion in the United States, more than an estimated 42 million babies have been aborted–and we are still counting.

Despite what many claim, the world is not getting better and better. When describing the end times, Jesus declared:

> And ye shall hear of wars and rumours of wars: see that ye be not troubled: for all these things must come to pass, but the end is not yet. For nation shall rise against nation, and kingdom against kingdom: and there shall be famines, and pestilences, and earthquakes, in divers places. All these are the beginning of sorrows. Then shall they deliver you up to be afflicted, and shall kill you: and ye shall be hated of all nations for my name's sake. And then shall many be offended, and shall betray one another, and shall hate one another. And many false prophets shall rise, and shall deceive many. And

because iniquity shall abound, the love of many shall wax cold.

Matthew 24:6-12

Under the inspiration of the Holy Spirit, Paul warned:

This know also, that in the last days perilous times shall come. For men shall be lovers of their own selves, covetous, boasters, proud, blasphemers, disobedient to parents, unthankful, unholy, Without natural affection, trucebreakers, false accusers, incontinent, fierce, despisers of those that are good, Traitors, heady, highminded, lovers of pleasures more than lovers of God; Having a form of godliness, but denying the power thereof: from such turn away. For of this sort are they which creep into houses, and lead captive silly women laden with sins, led away with divers lusts, Ever learning, and never able to come to the knowledge of the truth.

2 Timothy 3:1-7

The Apostle Peter also declared, *"Knowing this first, that there shall come in the last days scoffers, walking after their own lusts..."* (2 Peter 3:3).

The days of Elijah were times of moral, political, and spiritual degeneracy that mirror conditions in our world in these end times. Into this arena of spiritual, moral, and political conflict, Elijah enters with God-given power and authority with a direct word from the Lord God Jehovah, God of Abraham, Isaac, and Jacob. That word is drought. There will be no rain, no dew, no moisture of any kind for three years.

It is into a similar environment of moral, political, and spiritual degeneracy that our modern-day Elijahs will enter. Like Elijah, they must be bold. They must be anointed. They must be fearless and they must come with a powerful word from God in their mouths.

CHAPTER TWO

DECLARING THE WORD OF THE LORD

*A nd Elijah the Tishbite, who was of the inhabitants of Gilead,
said unto Ahab, As the Lord God of Israel liveth, before whom
I stand, there shall not be dew nor rain these years, but according to
my word.*

1 Kings 17:1

The Hebrews word for God is *Elohim*, which is sometimes abbreviated *El.*

The word "jah" is the word for *Jehovah*. Elijah's name contains the words for God and Jehovah, and between them is the small letter I, which in Hebrew means *"my or mine."* Putting this together, we find that Elijah's name means *"My God is Jehovah."*

We are told very little about Elijah. He is referred to only as *"Elijah the Tishbite"* (1 Kings 17:1). We know nothing about his ancestry, his parents, or his early life and we know very little about Tishbeh from where he came. We don't know its exact location, other than that it was in Gilead which was a place of solitude, a rocky, isolated, and rugged place, not a city of any great sophistication.

Elijah had no experience with court protocol and no formal training to be a prophet that we know of. He wore a garment of black camel's hair with a leather belt around his waist which was the official dress of Old Testament prophets (2 Kings 1:7-8; Zechariah 13:4). His manner and dress were symbolic of his priorities. Material things were not his focus. Protocol and platitudes were not his mission.

MODERN-DAY ELIJAHS

Like this prophet, the Elijahs that God is raising up throughout the world will not rely on their ancestry, their credentials, their education, or their denomination. They may not have formal ministry training. Their focus will not be on material possessions. Their focus will be on the priority of their God-given destiny.

Like Moses, these Elijahs will learn that it is not important who they are, it is only important who God is, Who has commissioned them, and the intimacy they have experienced with Him:

> And God said unto Moses, I AM THAT I AM: and he said, Thus shalt thou say unto the children of Israel, I AM hath sent me unto you.
>
> Exodus 3:14-15

The spirit of Elijah is an anointing to prophecy, to speak prophetically into the lives of men and nations. In our first encounter with Elijah, we find him boldly speaking forth the word of the Lord to evil King Ahab. Elijah declared: *"As the Lord God of Israel liveth, before whom I stand, there shall not be dew nor rain these years, but according to my word"* (1 Kings 17:1).

It was not a long message. It didn't have an introduction, three points, and a closing statement. There was no soft music at the end to encourage a response. It is not how long you talk, but what you have to say that matters in the destiny of men and nations. Are you speaking your words, your thoughts, and your ideas, or are you a spokesperson for the Lord?

ELIJAH'S MESSAGE

Elijah's message was brief, powerful, to the point, and delivered with the authority of Almighty God. Let us examine in detail this Word from the Lord.

"As the Lord God of Israel liveth..." Elijah's very name, which meant "My God is Jehovah", declared that God is not a God of the past, but of the present. He is God. He does live. The world seeks not more martyred saints, not more memorials to great leaders, but a living God who is active in the affairs of men and nations. This brief declaration reveals that Elijah was:

1. Convinced that God lived.
2. Courageous enough to declare Him God of Israel in opposition to the false gods of the day.
3. Cognizant of his position as a representative of God "before whom I stand."

If you want to minister in the spirit and power of Elijah, you, too must be convinced, courageous, and cognizant of your position as a representative of God.

"...before whom I stand..." Throughout biblical history, God sought men and women who would stand in the gap spiritually at strategic times: *"And I sought for a man among them, that should make up the hedge, and stand in the gap before me for the land, that I should not destroy it..."*(Ezekiel 22:30).

To stand in the gap means to intercede before God in behalf of others. A great example is Esther, who came into the Kingdom for "such a time as this." Consider Moses, who interceded for Israel when God would have destroyed them. Consider Deborah, who led an army to free God's people. Today, God is calling forth Elijahs all over this world–not mediocre, nominal, "secret service" Christians–but men and women who will be His messengers in this strategic time in history. These Elijahs will be men and women who will make a difference, powerful representatives who will not be afraid to stand alone for God. They will know who they are in God and function resolutely in that knowledge.

"...there shall not be dew nor rain these years, but according to my word." Elijah was a proof producer and the validity of his powerful, brief message would be proven through a dreadful drought. God's weather forecast for the next few years was not pleasant. Beneath burning skies and a searing sun, vegetation would die and people would succumb to thirst and hunger. Elijah used what I call prayer command faith–he simply declared, *"...there shall not be dew nor rain these years, but according to my word"* (1 Kings 17:1).

PRAYER COMMAND OF FAITH

Jesus illustrated this type of prayer with an incident involving a barren fruit true. One day, traveling on the way to Bethany, Jesus was hungry. He and his disciples passed a fig tree and, upon finding it barren, Jesus commanded, *"...No man eat fruit of thee hereafter for ever"* (Mark 11:12-14).

Jesus didn't pray a lengthy prayer. He didn't go into deep intercession. He simply commanded in faith.

The next day, as the group passed the tree again, they found it withered and dead. When Peter pointed this out, Jesus said,

> ...Have faith in God. For verily I say unto you, That whosoever shall say unto this mountain, Be thou removed, and be thou cast into the sea; and shall not doubt in his heart, but shall believe that those things which he saith shall come to pass; he shall have whatsoever he saith.

Mark 11:22-23

Jesus didn't curse the fig tree in a fit of anger because of its barrenness. He had a specific purpose in His actions. He used this tree to teach His disciples about prayer command faith. He told them the fig tree was simply an illustration of the type of faith that could command and move obstacles. This type of command is not indiscriminate asking, however. It must be in harmony with God's will, for He hears us if we ask according to His will (1 John 5:14-15).

Jesus said, *"Have faith in God."* It is not faith alone. It is not your faith. It is faith in God that causes mountains to move. Before you can speak to mountains with divine authority, you must have a faith relationship with God.

The Bible declares that we are saved by faith: *"For by grace are ye saved through faith; and that not of yourselves: it is the gift of God: Not of works, lest any man should boast" (Ephesians 2:8-9).*

We are saved by faith that is a gift of God. We are not saved by our own faith. Faith is a gift. It is the faith of God, not your faith that will enable you to embrace the Elijah anointing and walk in the demonstration of power.

Are you ready to rise up to this new dimension of prayer where you pray in faith and command mountains–obstacles, difficulties, and impossibilities–to move out of your way? What are the mountains standing between you and the fulfillment of God's will, His purpose, and plan for you? Is it...

- An incurable disease?
- Lack of income or a mountain of debt?
- Satanic strongholds?

These circumstances will move when you enter into the Elijah anointing. Begin to speak with prayer command faith to your circumstances and see those mountains move in Jesus' Name.

The first key to this experience is to speak God's words, as Jesus did. He declared:

> *Then said Jesus unto them, When ye have lifted up the Son of man, then shall ye know that I am he, and that I do nothing of myself; but as my Father hath taught me, I speak these things.*

> John 8:28

It is not your words, but God's Word in your mouth that will move mountains and speak into existence miracles.

The second key to this level of prayer is *"...and shall not doubt in his heart but believe..."* We must stop being double-minded in our prayers. Many Christians believe that God answers prayer, but how often do we pray and not really expect God to answer? We know God *can* do all things, but how often are you assured before you pray that He *will* answer your prayer?

There is one thing you must do when you pray: Believe. When did Jesus say you are to believe that you have received the things for which you have asked? After you have received them? No! He said when you pray, believe that you have received them. You may not actually see the answer manifested until later, but when you pray without having seen the answer in the natural–you are to believe that the Father has already answered.

Verse 24 summarizes the unlimited potential we have in this level of prayer. Jesus said, *"Therefore I say unto you, what things soever ye desire, when ye pray, believe that ye receive them, and ye shall have them"* (Mark 11:24).

This promise is so comprehensive that our natural minds immediately begin to place limitations on it. We begin to doubt and say, "This can't possibly be literally true." Jesus carefully chose His words and used the strongest expression He could find to explain the unlimited potential of prayer.

ALIGN YOURSELF WITH GOD'S PURPOSES

When Elijah appeared before wicked King Ahab, he did not give his own opinions or come up with his own thoughts or plans. Effective ministry is not coming up with your ideas and asking God to bless them, but it is in aligning yourself with the revealed will of God, speaking forth His Word, and boldly commanding that it be done.

Elijah didn't follow political protocol of being announced, bowing, and delivering pious platitudes. He knew God's will, he had God's Word in his mouth, and he declared God's purposes with power and authority. Years later, Jesus would speak in similar manner:

And it came to pass, when Jesus had ended these sayings, the people were astonished at his doctrine: For he taught them as one having authority , and not as the scribes.

Matthew 7:28-29

Jesus taught with power. His message was not the formal, dry recitation of the law.

His words were endued with the power of Almighty God. His message was one of power: "*And they were astonished at his doctrine: for his word was with power*" (Luke 4:32).

Jesus passed on this tremendous spiritual power to His followers for the specific purpose of accomplishing the task of reaching the world with the proof-producing Gospel message.

He declared:

> *And Jesus came and spake unto them, saying, All power is given unto me in heaven and in earth. Go ye therefore, and teach all nations, baptizing them in the name of the Father, and of the Son, and of the Holy Ghost: Teaching them to observe all things whatsoever I have commanded you: and, lo, I am with you alway, even unto the end of the world.*

Matthew 28:18-20

God is raising up Elijahs who will not just teach religious dogma, but who will deliver the Word of God in power and authority. They may not be great orators. Their grammar and linguistic abilities will not particularly matter. With power and authority they will deliver their message from God and the world will be astonished. The world is hungry to see the manifestation of God's power. The world is waiting in desperation for a message direct from God.

Right from the outset, we see that Elijah's ministry was received, not achieved. Paul declared in Colossians 4:17, "*...Take heed to the ministry which thou hast received in the Lord, that thou fulfil it.*" To be successful, a ministry must be received from God, not achieved through academic excellence or natural abilities and talents.

But remember: Just because a ministry is God-initiated doesn't mean it will be easy. As the Elijah generation arises, our purpose is not to amass wealth and enjoy the pleasures of life. We are representatives of the living God and we are called to do battle with Satanic forces for the souls of men and nations.

As we will see in the lives of Elijah and Elisha, it won't always be easy. Over the years I have survived coups, false accusations, riots, and imprisonment for the sake of the Gospel. This is why you must know your purpose. Your purpose will help you persevere. Your purpose will endue you with power. Your focus on God's revealed purpose will enable you to press on, despite the difficulties.

WHERE ARE THE PROPHETS?

As we will learn later in the story of Elijah, there were 7,000 other prophets of God during his time, but we read only of the exploits of Elijah. Many of these prophets were hiding in caves in fear for their lives.

Today, many believers are resting in their caves of comfort and materialism. There are multitudes who are afraid to step forth boldly and declare God's Word. They don't want to risk their lives or reputations.

The Elijahs that God is calling out today will come forth with a powerful Word in their mouths. They will not fear. They will not retreat. They will boldly march into the very pits of Hell to the unsaved, they will confront violent prison inmates, prostitutes, drug addicts, idolaters and adulterers and declare, "Thus saith the Lord!"

CHAPTER THREE

THE PLACE OF CUTTING

A nd the word of the Lord came unto him, saying, Get thee hence, and turn thee eastward, and hide thyself by the brook Cherith, that is before Jordan. And it shall be, that thou shalt drink of the brook; and I have commanded the ravens to feed thee there. So he went and did according unto the word of the Lord: for he went and dwelt by the brook Cherith, that is before Jordan. And the ravens brought him bread and flesh in the morning, and bread and flesh in the evening; and he drank of the brook.

1 Kings 17:2-4

What matters most in your life and ministry is not what you hear from the pulpit, read in a book, or hear on a tape or CD. As an Elijah, it is vital that you are able to hear from God because *"....the way of man is not in himself: it is not in man that walketh to direct his steps"* (Jeremiah 10:23).

Sometimes–in fact most often–God's way doesn't make sense in the natural and the reason for this is quite clear:

For my thoughts are not your thoughts, neither are your ways my ways, saith the Lord. For as the heavens are higher than the earth, so are my ways higher than your ways, and my thoughts than your thoughts.

Isaiah 55:8-9

Settle it in your heart: As you walk in the spirit and power of Elijah, the ways in which God leads you will not always make sense. Here is a vital biblical key that will keep you in the center of God's will:

Trust in the Lord with all thine heart; and lean not unto thine own understanding. In all thy ways acknowledge him, and he shall direct thy paths.

Proverbs 3:5-6

Even when God's way doesn't seem to make sense, you can be assured that divine design is in process:

And we know that all things work together for good to them that love God, to them who are the called according to his purpose. For whom he did foreknow, he also did predestinate to be conformed to the image of his Son, that he might be the firstborn among many brethren. Moreover whom he did predestinate, them he also called: and whom he called, them he also justified: and whom he justified, them he also glorified.

Romans 8:28-30

God usually guides a step at a time. We want the whole route. We want a complete itinerary and a "career path." But that is not the way God works. We will see in the life of Elijah that God shows the prophet only one move at a time.

GO TO CHERITH

Immediately after his powerful declaration to Ahab, Elijah heard the word of the Lord again. This time, it directed him to go to the Brook Cherith and remain there, Now remember, Elijah had just emerged as a prophet and delivered a powerful message in 1 Kings 17:1. Now God is telling him to withdraw from public ministry and go to the Brook Cherith. The word "Cherith" means "isolation or to cut off, a place of cutting." It may have obtained the name by a deep ravine cut through the rocks by the water flow over the years. It was a place of isolation and seclusion.

Elijah could have refused to go. He might have argued, "I am a prophet, sent to the nations. I am wasting my time, my talents, and my gifts here. The nation needs me!" Instead, he obeyed the word of the Lord. God seeks modern-day Elijahs who will go or stay at God's command, whether it makes sense or not, whether it be seclusion or in the spotlight.

In New Testament times, the evangelist Philip was conducting a tremendously successful campaign in Samaria (Acts 8). Miracles were occurring–the lame walking, the deaf hearing, demonic spirits coming out of those who were bound. The entire city was being impacted. Yet, in the midst of this tremendous revival, the Holy Spirit directed Philip to go to a stretch of desert between Gaza and Jerusalem (Acts 8:26).

Although it didn't make sense in the natural to leave this fruitful ministry and retreat to the desert, Philip obeyed and it was there that he encountered the Ethiopian eunuch and led him to the Lord. Many theologians believe that this man was responsible for the subsequent spread of the Gospel to all of Africa.

Like Elijah and Philip, you must be prepared for radical, paradigm shifts. Your mind will tell you to go one way, but the Holy Spirit will direct you another and your obedience, like that of Philip, may determine the destiny of entire continents.

WHERE GOD GUIDES, HE PROVIDES

At Cherith, God provided for Elijah through natural means (the brook) and supernatural means (the ravens). As you minister in the anointing of Elijah, you will learn that where God guides, He will always provide. Sometimes it will be through natural means, sometimes through the supernatural, but you can be assured, *"...my God shall supply all your need according to his riches in glory by Christ Jesus"* (Philippians 4:19).

Ravens were sent by God to feed Elijah. In biblical times, ravens were regarded as omens of misfortune, death, or tragedy and were unclean because of their scavenger habits.

God chose unclean birds to feed His prophet! Let me ask you this: Are you willing to trust God even if what He does is contrary to your preconceived ideas? As an Elijah, God will use all kinds of instruments, people, and circumstances to propel you into your destiny. Don't get your eyes on the instruments He uses. Keep your eyes on Jehovah-Jireh, the God who supplies your needs.

Do you have to be in the spotlight all the time? Do you constantly need the cheers of the crowd? If so, then you may not be cut out to be an Elijah. Cherith was God's place of divine appointment for Elijah, for there in solitude he would be prepared for his destiny. This was not a vacation. Elijah didn't just spend the weekend. He lived there. Are you willing to be set aside for a season, to tarry in the presence of God until endued with power to impact nations?

WAITING ON GOD

Getting alone with God is not optional. When we spend time with God in seclusion, we come to know His purposes and plans and our ministry becomes more effective. In our spiritual Cherith, we feed on the provisions of His Word and drink from the streams of living water.

There are eight words used in the Bible for wait and their combined meanings are "to await or expect eagerly; look for, look for with a view to favorable reception; tarry; continue steadfastly; sit constantly beside, patiently waiting."

The Bible is filled with examples of those who waited on God.

- Noah waited 120 years before the rain came in fulfillment of God's prophetic word (Genesis 7:6).

- At the age of 75, Abraham was promised a new land, but waited many years to see the promise fulfilled (Genesis 17:5).

- Esther waited one night, and saved the Jews (Esther 5:7).

- Joseph endured at least two to three years inside an Egyptian prison for a crime he didn't commit, but then emerged as leader of the land (Genesis 41:1).

- Moses waited 40 years in the wilderness before returning to Egypt to deliver God's people (Acts 7:30).

- Paul, after his conversion, spent three years in seclusion growing in the knowledge of the Lord (Galatians 1:18).

- The disciples waited in the Upper Room 10 days until endued with the power of the Holy Spirit (Acts 1-2).

- It is estimated that Jesus was in seclusion for some 30 years until the fullness of time in God's plan for Him to begin His ministry.

There are numerous commands in Scripture to wait on the Lord:

"Wait on the Lord: be of good courage, and he shall strengthen thine heart: wait, I say, on the Lord" Psalm 27:14.

Rest in the Lord, and wait patiently for him... Psalm 37:7.

Wait on the Lord, and keep his way, and he shall exalt thee to inherit the land... Psalm 37:34.

Your waiting is never wasted. It is invested. The time Elijah spent at the brook was not wasted. It was a time of preparation as he prayed, communed with God, and waited before Him to hear His voice.

To be able to hear God's voice and be led by His Spirit, you must take time to be alone with Him and learn to hear the still small voice of His Spirit speaking to you. Your ability to hear and discern God's voice is the single most important thing in your life. You must be willing to shut out all distractions and wait upon Him. God wants to speak to you in ways you have never experienced, but your ears must be sensitized by the Holy Spirit. This happens as you develop an intimate relationship with Him in seclusion.

BEARING THE MARKS OF CHANGE

Remember the meaning of the word Cherith? It means "cutting." Cherith is a place of "cutting," where God removes sins, bad habits, and negative attitudes, etc.

When Moses was on his way to deliver God's people from slavery, the angel of the Lord stopped him because he had not been circumcised (Exodus 4:24-26). Circumcision was instituted by God during the time of Abraham as a token of His covenant with His people. Before Moses could affect the lives of others, the marks of change must be upon him. He could not deliver God's people without the marks of the covenant upon his own life. After his circumcision, Moses was mobilized to do a mighty work for God.

To minister to others and to pass on the mantle of the anointing, your life must first bear the marks of change.

Joshua 5:2-9 records the story of when the children of Israel entered the promised land. There, in the very shadow of the enemy, God commanded all the males to be circumcised as a token of the covenant between them and God. Circumcision had not been practiced during the wilderness wandering and the new generation of Israelites did not bear the sign of the covenant upon them. Israel was preparing to war against the nations of Canaan, yet at this time, God commanded them to be circumcised, to voluntarily disable themselves in the presence of the enemy.

A ministers of God we must bear the marks of change upon our lives. As believers, we no longer circumcise the flesh, but we must be circumcised in heart:

> In whom also ye are circumcised with the circumcision made without hands, in putting off the body of the sins of the flesh by the circumcision of Christ.

> Colossians 2:11

Our circumcision is spiritual; of the heart instead of the flesh. But if you have been circumcised in heart, there will be external signs just as when Israel circumcised its flesh. You will act, talk, and live differently. Your life will bear the marks of change which are the signs of your covenant with God:

> *For he is not a Jew which is one outwardly; neither is that circumcision which is outward of the flesh: But he is a Jew which is one inwardly; and circumcision is that of the heart, in the spirit, and not in the letter; whose praise is not of men, but of God.*

Romans 2:28-29

If you are to walk in the spirit and power of Elijah, you must first visit "Cherith," the place of cutting. Your own life must bear the marks of supernatural change. Do not be afraid of the "knife" of God's Word as it marks your life. The reproach of Egypt (sin) must be rolled away and you must put off the filth of the flesh.

Like Israel, as you camp in the very shadow of your enemy, you must realize that you cannot war in the flesh. You must disable your flesh and trust only in the power of Almighty God. The land will be penetrated and possessed only by weakness of the flesh and in the power of the Spirit.

This circumcision of heart is twofold.

• God has a part in it: *"And the Lord thy God will circumcise thine heart..."* (Deuteronomy 30:6).

• You have a part in it: *"Circumcise yourselves to the Lord, and take away the foreskins of your heart..."* (Jeremiah 4:4).

God changes your life and makes you a new creature, but you must continually cleanse yourself of the filthiness of the flesh. You cannot do your part until He does His part because that would be an attempt at self-improvement. But you must do your part! If you are to minister under the Elijah anointing, then you must rid yourself of immorality, dishonesty, anger, bitterness, unforgiveness, addictions, and filthy habits.

You must have the mark of God upon your life.

CHERITH MUST PRECEDE CARMEL

Cherith–the cutting–must precede Carmel.

If we are to go to the next level in God, we cannot reject the "cutting experiences," the times of isolation and seclusion. These times, though painful, prepare us for the mountain-top experiences. Cherith equips us to stand before entire nations. Cherith prepares us to emerge with the authority of Almighty God and confront the evils of our world.

I believe that all around this world there are mighty men and women of God who have wondered why they are in a place of difficulty, hidden away, isolated, and secluded. God has placed you there for the same reasons He sent Elijah to Cherith: For preparation.

You will never minister to a nation, as Elijah did on Mt. Carmel, until you have first learned the lessons of Cherith.

CHAPTER FOUR

WHEN THE BROOK RUNS DRY

*A*nd it came to pass after a while, that the brook dried up, because there had been no rain in the land. And the word of the Lord came unto him, saying, Arise, get thee to Zarephath, which belongeth to Zidon, and dwell there: behold, I have commanded a widow woman there to sustain thee.

1 Kings 17:7-9

The brook ran dry. Whether by natural processes of the drought or supernatural intervention, it was the outworking of a sovereign God. As the Elijah generation, we must learn that the circumstances–whether natural or supernatural–that affect us are not about us but are about God's purposes.

When God first directed Elijah to the Brook Cherith, He provided for him miraculously. Ravens fed him and the brook provided fresh water in a time when the nation was experiencing drought and famine. But eventually, the brook dried up. Why would God send Elijah to a brook that He knew would dry up?

If we are to walk in the spirit and power of Elijah, we must learn how to deal with dry brooks. You will encounter them many times during your ministry. When you do, don't fret. Don't wring your hands in despair. Just know that a change is coming.

Elijah had not missed the will of God when he went to Cherith. The Lord led him to the brook and for some time, Elijah had enjoyed its waters. His needs were provided. He was blessed of God. But when it was time to move on, God allowed the brook to dry up. Spiritual timing is vital to the move of God. It is the key to spiritual harvest. We must be prepared to move when God says move.

BE PREPARED FOR DRY BROOKS

God's timing is usually not ours, so you must be prepared for sudden changes. I am sure Elijah would have lingered at Cherith, had not the brook run dry. But God had another plan for provision.

Never get caught up with the methods, means, or things God supplies. Your focus must be on God alone. He is your provider, He is in control, and He is working everything together for His purposes.

The words "dried up" in the King James version refers to a process. Elijah didn't just wake up one morning and find the brook gone. Day by day, he saw it dwindling. Do you think he measured the brook each day? You cannot measure what God is doing. You cannot understand the supernatural with carnal reasoning or statistics.

Perhaps God has directed you to a "Brook Cherith" in your life and ministry. You know you heard His voice of direction and at first He greatly blessed you at your brook. Your needs were met and you rejoiced in God's blessings. You learned the lessons He had for you.

But now, the brook is running dry. Maybe you no longer experience the flow of God's power. Perhaps people have turned against you. Perhaps leadership above you has dammed up the brook and stopped the flow. For whatever reason, your beautiful brook is dry.

When the brook runs dry, you can do one of two things:

1. You can sit on the bank spiritually speaking and complain about your fate. You can spend the rest of your life wondering why it happened and weeping over the dry creek bed. You can question the leading of God. If He knew the brook was going to run dry, why would He have brought you here? Did you miss God's will?

Or. . .

2. You can realize that as surely as God brought you to this brook, He is now ready to move you on to a new dimension of His will.

Drying brooks gain our attention. Drying brooks prepare us for the next move of God.

If brooks never dried up–if God never let difficult times come–we would settle right where we are and never move on to new things. We would never stray beyond the banks of security of our little brook.

ARE YOU FACING A DRYING BROOK?

Some of you are facing drying brooks right now. This book did not fall into your hands by accident. God wants you to know that He is aware of the drying brook of your circumstances or your ministry. Don't lament over the drying brook. Don't give up. Don't remain by the dry creek bed. If you will receive this revelation of the drying brook, God will use it to catapult you to the next level.

Drying brooks lead to greater things. Before the experience at Cherith, Elijah ministered only to individuals. After this faith-building encounter at Cherith, Elijah ministered to multitudes. He stood on Mt. Carmel and proclaimed before a nation of idolaters that God was the true and living God.

When you face drying brooks, your faith must not fail. You are on the banks of receiving new revelation from God. Do not question that dry creek bed. Get up, pack up your gear, and move on to the next dimension of God's plan.

CHAPTER FIVE

INTO THE CRUCIBLE

It wasn't until the brook ran dry that God revealed to Elijah the next step in His plan. God directed Elijah to go to the city of Zarephath which means "smelting, refining, and testing."

> *So he arose and went to Zarephath. And when he came to the gate of the city, behold, the widow woman was there gathering of sticks: and he called to her, and said, Fetch me, I pray thee, a little water in a vessel, that I may drink. And as she was going to fetch it, he called to her, and said, Bring me, I pray thee, a morsel of bread in thine hand. And she said, As the Lord thy God liveth, I have not a cake, but an handful of meal in a barrel, and a little oil in a cruse: and, behold, I am gathering two sticks, that I may go in and dress it for me and my son, that we may eat it, and die. And Elijah said unto her, Fear not; go and do as thou hast said: but make me thereof a little cake first, and bring it unto me, and after make for thee and for thy son. For thus saith the Lord God of Israel, The barrel of meal shall not waste, neither shall the cruse of oil fail, until the day that the Lord sendeth rain upon the earth. And she went and did according to the saying of Elijah: and she, and he, and her house, did eat many days. And the barrel of meal wasted not, neither did the cruse of oil fail, according to the word of the Lord, which he spake by Elijah.*

> 1 Kings 17:10-16

Zarephath was a hostile environment, as the city was located in the center of Baal worship. Being sent there meant going into enemy territory.

God is calling Elijahs all over this world to step out of the safety of obscurity, tradition, and custom into enemy territory. Some of you will leave the security of your own homes and nations to go into regions hostile to the Gospel. Like Elijah, God may direct you to the very heart of enemy territory.

ARISE, GO, STAY

God said to Elijah, "Arise, go, and stay there." God is directing Elijahs all over this world to "arise" and to "go" to their "Zarepaths" –difficult places of refining, testing, and spiritual warfare. It is one thing to arise and go into the difficult environments of this world, but it is quite another to stay there. As an Elijah, you must have staying power, the ability to stick it out when thing get tough, when the times of testing and refining come.

The first challenge Elijah faced in Zarephath was provision. Remember, there had been a famine in the land for some time now due to the lack of rain. God told Elijah that his provision would come through a widow woman. This was highly irregular, for it was the custom of the day for a man to be the provider. This woman was also a Gentile of the pagan nation of Sidon, and the Jews looked down on Gentiles. In addition, she was poor, destitute, and facing starvation.

Sometimes God uses the powerful and wealthy as in the case of Nehemiah (Nehemiah 2) or Joseph in the later chapters of Genesis. Other times, God chooses to use unconventional means. What is most important is that you look beyond the instrument God uses to the real source of your supply: God.

When the command came to go to Zarepath, Elijah arose, went, and stayed at the direction of the Lord. There were no questions ("Why?"), complaints ("Live off a widow? You've got to be kidding!"), or arguments ("This woman is a poor widow and a Gentile!").

When Elijah arrived at Zarepath, he met a widow woman gathering sticks for her fire because she had no money for fuel. She also had little food–just enough for one more meal:

> *And she said, As the Lord thy God liveth, I have not a cake, but an handful of meal in a barrel, and a little oil in a cruse: and, behold, I am gathering two sticks, that I may go in and dress it for me and my son, that we may eat it, and die.*

1 Kings 17:12

YOU WILL BE SENT TO SIMILAR PEOPLE

This woman had given up. She was ready to die. As you minister in the spirit and power of Elijah, these are the types of people to whom God will send you. They will be poor. They will be hopeless and ready to give up. They will be spiritually dying. Into the shambles of their lives, you will come with a word from God that will change their circumstances.

When our own natural resources are exhausted and we are at the point of our greatest need, then we are poised for a miracle. Elijah told this woman not to fear and directed her to take her remaining oil and flour, prepare food for him first, and then prepare a meal for her family.

In your life and ministry, your "flour and oil" may represent your own limited financial resources: Your paycheck, your small church with limited funds, your bank account. If you keep your eyes on these, you will hinder what God wants to do in your life and ministry. Get your eyes off of your limited resources and on to an unlimited God.

Anything, when placed in God's hands, can be transformed not only to meet our needs, but the needs of those around us. In New Testament times, a young boy with five loaves of bread and two fish placed his meager resources into the Master's hands and a multitude was fed (Matthew 14:17-21).

It is not the resources you possess—your money, talents, and abilities—but it is what you do with them that is important. Do you selfishly horde what you have, or do you give it into the hands of the Master?

Elijah directed the woman not to fear, but to do as he asked, to make a meal for him and then provide for her family:

> And Elijah said unto her, Fear not; go and do as thou hast said: but make me thereof a little cake first, and bring it unto me, and after make for thee and for thy son.

> 1 Kings 17:3

After the woman had obeyed the directions of the Prophet Elijah, then he gave her God's promise:

> For thus saith the Lord God of Israel, The barrel of meal shall not waste, neither shall the cruse of oil fail, until the day that the Lord sendeth rain upon the earth.

> 1 Kings 17:14

The widow responded in faith to Elijah's directions. She built a fire, baked a cake for Elijah, and then prepared a meal for herself and her son. In response to her obedient faith, just as God promised, the jar of flour and the jug of oil did not run dry. Each day, as the widow reached down into the jar for flour and poured the oil to prepare food, it multiplied.

TOTAL PROVISION, CONTINUAL SUPPLY

What this widow experienced was the supernatural provision of God: Total provision, continual supply. She learned to depend on God for daily provision. God did not prosper her by a large sum of money or filling her cupboards with enough food to last throughout the famine, although He could have easily done these things. Instead, He supplied for her day by day.

God will supply adequate resources for you even in the time of financial famine. The word of the Lord to you today is the same that Elijah spoke to the widow: "Fear not!" Look to God as your Source, give out of your need, and then get ready! The same supernatural God who multiplied the flour and oil will supply your personal needs and those of your family and your ministry. You can feed on God's miracle provision each day, and it will never run out.

God will raise up from your own country, out of your own resources, the funds necessary for you to accomplish His will. I have taught this for years on the foreign fields, and those who have grasped this revelation have found it to be true.

Look to God to meet your needs. Look to Him to provide the funds to fulfill your vision and teach this to the Elishas you train. Don't look to your denomination. Don't look to man. Take what you have and place it in His hands, and get ready for a miracle.

A GOD-DIRECTED MINISTRY

Before we leave this story, I want to stress another great truth in this account. It is the fact that Elijah's ministry was God-directed, not people directed. Jesus declares in Luke 4:25-27:

> But I tell you of a truth, many widows were in Israel in the days of Elias, when the heaven was shut up three years and six months, when great famine was throughout all the land; But unto none of them was Elias sent, save unto Sarepta, a city of Sidon, unto a woman that was a widow. And many lepers were in Israel in the time of Eliseus the prophet; and none of them was cleansed, saving Naaman the Syrian.

There were many widows, but Elijah was sent to only one. Later on, there were many lepers, but Elisha was sent to one. Both men were God-directed instead of people-directed. There were other widows and other

lepers, but they didn't let the needs of people control them. They were God-controlled. They went only where God sent them. If your ministry is God-directed, it will be God-controlled. If your ministry is people-directed, it will be people-controlled. The choice is yours.

CHAPTER SIX

PRODUCING THE PROOF

A nd it came to pass after these things, that the son of the woman, the mistress of the house, fell sick; and his sickness was so sore, that there was no breath left in him. And she said unto Elijah, What have I to do with thee, O thou man of God? art thou come unto me to call my sin to remembrance, and to slay my son? And he said unto her, Give me thy son. And he took him out of her bosom, and carried him up into a loft, where he abode, and laid him upon his own bed. And he cried unto the Lord, and said, O Lord my God, hast thou also brought evil upon the widow with whom I sojourn, by slaying her son? And he stretched himself upon the child three times, and cried unto the Lord, and said, O Lord my God, I pray thee, let this child's soul come into him again. And the Lord heard the voice of Elijah; and the soul of the child came into him again, and he revived. And Elijah took the child, and brought him down out of the chamber into the house, and delivered him unto his mother: and Elijah said, See, thy son liveth. And the woman said to Elijah, Now by this I know that thou art a man of God, and that the word of the Lord in thy mouth is truth.

1 Kings 17:17-24

This passage opens with the words, *"And it came to pass after these things..."* After what things? After the Prophet Elijah had come to dwell with the poor widow woman of Zarephath and God had miraculously met her needs through the continuing cycle of provision of flour and oil. After this, there came a day when the woman's son fell sick and died.

As so many of us do in times of trouble, this woman was immediately filled with questioning and guilt. Why hadn't the man of God intervened and her son been spared? Was this terrible thing a result of her previous sin? Despair, anger, and blame–all common reactions of those who suffer. The most deadly reaction, however, is shame–guilt over past sins and feeling like God is punishing you because of them.

We need to understand the root cause of this emotion called shame. Shame originated in the Garden of Eden after sin entered the universe. Adam and Eve hid themselves because they were fearful and ashamed of their nakedness (Genesis 3:10). These two emotions are the roots for all other negative emotions. Anger, bitterness, resentments–a host of negative reactions stem from fear and shame.

Shame drives you on a hunting expedition into your past, scrutinizing everything you have done wrong and building a case against you like an aggressive prosecutor in a court of law. Many reading these pages can readily identify with this description because "court" is in session daily in your own mind. The prosecutor raises the issue of:

> ...Your failed marriage.
> ...An aborted or abandoned child.
> ...Past criminal or sinful actions.

Relentlessly, the internal interrogation continues.

As an Elijah, you must communicate to people that shame is not of God. Satan is the accuser of the brethren (Revelation 12:10). Godly sorrow leads to repentance. Constructive sorrow produces a positive change and then it vanishes because its purpose is accomplished, but shame produces misery, lingering discouragement, and acute emotional pain.

The Apostle Paul declared that we should look...

> *...unto Jesus the author and finisher of our faith; who for the joy that was set before him endured the cross, despising the shame, and is set down at the right hand of the throne of God.*

Hebrews 12:2

To release people from the shackles of shame, you must declare to them that Jesus not only bore sin and sickness on the cross, He also bore shame. He died for your shame. In fact, of all He bore to the cross–the sin, the sickness–it was shame that He despised the most because He realized the devastating effects of this negative emotion.

If you are to deliver others from the power of shame, then you must first deal with it in your own life. Not only will this emotion keep you discouraged, but shame will interfere with your prayer life and affect your ministry. Perseverance is "shameless persistence." If you are filled with shame, you will be unable to persevere in prayer for yourself or others to receive an answer.

GIVE ME YOUR SON

In the face of this woman's questions and accusations, Elijah did not try to justify himself, debate with her, defend God, or delve into a theological treatise on the reasons for suffering. That is not Elijah's strategy for dealing with those in pain and suffering, nor should it be ours. We do not have to defend God or explain away circumstances. We don't need to have all the answers to questions from those who are suffering.

Elijah simply said, "Give me your son." When confronted with human suffering, we must do exactly what Elijah did. We must say:

- Give me your dead marriage.
- Give me your dead ministry.
- Give me your impossible situation.
- Give me your broken heart.
- Give me your bitterness, anger, and unforgiveness.

Then, as Elijah, we take the myriad of human suffering and needs into the inner chamber and lay the dead corpse of broken lives, marriages, and hearts before the Lord.

Elijah took the dead body of the widow's son to his own chamber where he regularly prayed and communed with the Father. Do you have an inner chamber where you commune regularly with God? Do you come daily into the inner court of His Presence? Without the inner court, there will be no outer court manifestations.

The law of Moses forbade priests from touching the dead (Leviticus 21:1-4), yet Elijah took this boy in his arms, carried him to his room, laid him on the bed, and stretched himself on him three times. He totally identified with this dead boy. Don't be afraid to get your hands dirty for God. Go to the prostitute, the drug addict, and the prison inmate. Stretch yourself out of your comfort zone and embrace these spiritually dead souls with the resurrecting power of an Almighty God.

At first, Elijah did not understand why God had allowed the boy to die. This prayer wasn't an expression of Elijah's doubt. It was simply his honest heartfelt cry. Elijah knew God intimately. Elijah wasn't afraid to ask God the tough questions.

He had developed that kind of intimate relationship with Him:

And he cried unto the Lord, and said, O Lord my God, hast thou also brought evil upon the widow with whom I sojourn, by slaying her son?

1 Kings 17:20

But Elijah didn't stop with questioning:

...he stretched himself upon the child three times, and cried unto the Lord, and said, O Lord my God, I pray thee, let this child's soul come into him again. And the Lord heard the voice of Elijah; and the soul of the child came into him again, and he revived.

1 Kings 17:21-22

As an act of faith, Elijah stretched himself upon the child three times and cried, "...*O Lord my God, I pray thee, let this child's soul come into him again*" (1 Kings 17:21).

Elijah did not pray a long, drawn-out prayer. His prayer was simple and direct. It was a prayer of faith based upon his personal knowledge of Almighty God.

Three times Elijah stretched himself out over the lifeless body of the boy and prayed for life to flow into him. This may sound like a strange thing to do, but there was such a flow of God's power in Elijah that as he covered the boy's body, the life of God flowed through him into the lad.

The answer did not come at once. The first time Elijah stretched himself over the young man, nothing happened. The second time he stretched out upon the boy he prayed, "O Lord my God let this boy's life return to him!" Nothing happened. It wasn't until after the third time he stretched himself out upon the boy that God heard his cry. "*The Lord heard Elijah's cry, and the boy's life returned to him, and he lived*" (1 Kings 17:22 NIV). The power of death was broken through effectual, fervent prayer.

YOU WILL DO NEW THINGS

The Elijah spirit views obstacles as opportunities for God to demonstrate His power and doesn't retreat in the face of impossibilities. To this point in the biblical record, there was no instance of the dead being resurrected. Elijah had no guide book for raising the dead.

As you minister in the spirit and power of Elijah, you will do things for which there is no precedence. You won't have a book on "Seven Steps to Raise the Dead," a seminar to train you, or a manual to guide you. You will have to launch out by faith and do new things:

> *Remember ye not the former things, neither consider the things of old. Behold I will do a new thing; now it shall spring forth; shall ye not know it?...Behold, the former things are come to pass, and new things do I declare: before they spring forth I tell you of them.*

Isaiah 42:9

From the beginning of time, God the Creator did new things (Genesis 1). In the closing pages of the Word we find Him still doing new things, creating a new heaven and earth and making all things new (Revelation 21:1-5). Always be open to the new things of God.

Here is just a sampling of the "new things" God wants to do:

- Make us new creatures in Christ: "*Therefore if any man be in Christ, he is a new creature: old things are passed away; behold, all things are become new*" (2 Corinthians 5:17).

- Lead us in new ways: "*Having therefore, brethren, boldness to enter into the holiest by the blood of Jesus. By a new and living way which he hath consecrated for us, through the vail, that is to say, His flesh*" (Hebrews 10:19-20).

- Give us a new spirit and a new heart: "*A new heart also will I give you, and a new spirit will I put within you; and I will take away the stony heart out of your flesh, and I will give you an heart of flesh. And I will put my spirit within you...*" (Ezekiel 36:26-27).

- Give us a new mind: "*And have put on the new man, which is renewed in knowledge after the image of him that created him*" (Colossians 3:10).

- Give us new thoughts: "*For my thoughts are not your thoughts, neither are your ways my ways, saith the Lord. For as the heavens are higher than the earth, so are my ways higher than your ways, and my thoughts than your thoughts*" (Isaiah 55:8-9).

- Provide us a new model: *"But we all, with open face beholding as in a glass the glory of the Lord, are changed into the same image from glory to glory, even as by the Spirit of the Lord"* (2 Corinthians 3:18).

- Give a new song: *"Sing unto him a new song; play skillfully with a loud noise"* (Psalms 33:3).

- Extend new mercies: *"This I recall to mind, therefore have I hope. It is of the Lord's mercies that we are not consumed, because his compassions fail not. They are new every morning; great is thy faithfulness..."* (Lamentations 3:21-23).

- Reveal new things: *"I have shown thee new things from this time, even hidden things and thou didst not know them..."* (Isaiah 48:6).

This brief compilation of Scriptures illustrates that God is continually doing new things.

If Elijah had not been open to new things from God, he would have simply accepted the death of this child and tried to comfort the mother as best he could. But Elijah knew that nothing was impossible with God and that the things that were impossible to man were still possible with God (Jeremiah 32:17-27; Luke 1:37; Luke 18:27).

He stretched himself upon the child and prayed. One time. Two times. Three times...and God heard his appeal and life came into the child.

Visualize the joy on this mother's face as Elijah comes slowly down the stairs and places her son into her arms, alive and well:

And Elijah took the child, and brought him down out of the chamber into the house, and delivered him unto his mother: and Elijah said, See, thy son liveth. And the woman said to Elijah, Now by this I know that thou art a man of God, and that the word of the Lord in thy mouth is truth.

1 Kings 17:23-24

When Elijah brought the boy to his mother, she told him, *"...Now by this I know that thou art a man of God, and that the word of the Lord in thy mouth is truth"* (1 Kings 17:24). You see, it wasn't just Elijah's words that identified him as a prophet of the God of Israel. It wasn't the way he dressed or his manner of speaking. It was the power of God demonstrated through him as he walked in intimate relationship with God.

Elijah was a proof producer. The miracles produced the proof that God was who He said He was. It verified both the message and the messenger.

WORKING THE WORKS OF GOD

In the New Testament, the disciples came to Jesus asking, *"...What shall we do, that we might work the works of God?"* (John 6:28). The future of the Kingdom of God is in the hands of those who find the answer to this question, those who enter into the double-portion, proof-producing power of God. Look at your hands. God is asking, "Where are the Elijahs of God?"

To minister in the spirit and power of Elijah, you must go beyond the point of blessings, beyond goose bumps, beyond dancing, shouting, and spiritual emotion. You must enter the realm of the supernatural, proof-producing power of God. You must learn to take the limits off of God. You must learn to do as His Word directs. Pray for the sick. Cast out devils. Believe for the miraculous and see it manifested before your very eyes.

Get ready to receive the mantle, and be used by God to intervene in the circumstances of your city, your government, and your nation!

When Elijah placed the son into his mother's arms, he simply declared, "Here he is alive..." He didn't say, "See what I did!" The miracles are not your miracles. The miracles were not Moses' miracles, Elijah's miracles, Elisha's miracles, or those of the disciples. The miracles are God's miracles. They are the manifestation of the double-portion anointing flowing through your life to impact a lost and dying world.

This anointing was not just for Elijah. It is not just for Morris Cerullo. It is also for you, the Elijah generation:

> *And when he had called unto him his twelve disciples, he gave them power against unclean spirits, to cast them out, and to heal all manner of sickness and all manner of disease.*

> Matthew 10:1

> *And Jesus came and spake unto them, saying, All power is given unto*

*me in heaven and in earth. Go ye therefore, and teach all nations,
baptizing them in the name of the Father, and of the Son, and of the
Holy Ghost: Teaching them to observe all things whatsoever I have
commanded you: and, lo, I am with you alway, even unto the end
of the world.*

Matthew 28:18-20

Some people maintain that this type of spiritual power was only for the
early church. They say it was only for the disciples. They claim that the day
of miracles is past. But consider this question: Has the entire world been
reached with the Gospel? The task Jesus left His followers is no where close
to being finished.

We still have the responsibility of reaching the world with the Gospel
of the Kingdom. Jesus would not withdraw the authority and power before
the responsibility was fulfilled.

Read the story of the death and resurrection of Lazarus in John 11.
When Jesus arrived after Lazarus had died, Martha met Him and said: "...
Lord, if thou hadst been here, my brother had not died" (John 11:21). Jesus
said to her, " *Thy brother shall rise again*" (John 11:23). Martha said, "...*I
know that he shall rise again in the resurrection at the last day*" (John 11:24).
Then Jesus said to her:... "*I Am the resurrection, and the life; He that believeth
in me, though he were dead, yet shall he live*" (John 11:25).

Martha believed Jesus could have raised Lazarus in the past ("... *if thou
hadst been here*"). She believed Jesus would raise him in the future ("*at the
last day*"). But Jesus shared a very important truth with her. He said "*I Am*"
the resurrection and life. "*I Am*" is speaking in the present tense. Then He
raised Lazarus from the dead.

There is no such thing as a day of miracles. We serve a God of miracle
working power. In every age there is power to work miracles to meet the
needs of people. In every era and age, God is manifesting His power. His
word to you is, "*I Am*"–present tense.

The day of miracles is not past. It didn't stop with Elijah. It didn't stop
with Elisha. The day of miracles *is* today.

PRODUCING THE PROOF

CHAPTER SEVEN

BEARING THE PROPHET'S MESSAGE

And it came to pass after many days, that the word of the Lord came to Elijah in the third year, saying, Go, shew thyself unto Ahab; and I will send rain upon the earth. And Elijah went to shew himself unto Ahab. And there was a sore famine in Samaria. And Ahab called Obadiah, which was the governor of his house. (Now Obadiah feared the Lord greatly: For it was so, when Jezebel cut off the prophets of the Lord, that Obadiah took an hundred prophets, and hid them by fifty in a cave, and fed them with bread and water.) And Ahab said unto Obadiah, Go into the land, unto all fountains of water, and unto all brooks: peradventure we may find grass to save the horses and mules alive, that we lose not all the beasts. So they divided the land between them to pass throughout it: Ahab went one way by himself, and Obadiah went another way by himself. And as Obadiah was in the way, behold, Elijah met him: and he knew him, and fell on his face, and said, Art thou that my Lord Elijah? And he answered him, I am: go, tell thy Lord, Behold, Elijah is here. And he said, What have I sinned, that thou wouldest deliver thy servant into the hand of Ahab, to slay me? As the Lord thy God liveth, there is no nation or kingdom, whither my Lord hath not sent to seek thee: and when they said, He is not there; he took an oath of the kingdom and nation, that they found thee not. And now thou sayest, Go, tell thy Lord, Behold, Elijah is here. And it shall come to pass, as soon as I am gone from thee, that the Spirit of the Lord shall carry thee whither I know not; and so when I come and tell Ahab, and he cannot find thee, he shall slay me: but I thy servant fear the Lord from my youth. Was it not told my Lord what I did when Jezebel slew the prophets of the Lord, how I hid an hundred men of the Lord's prophets by fifty in a cave, and fed them with bread and water? And now thou sayest, Go, tell thy Lord, Behold, Elijah is here: and he shall slay me. And Elijah said, As the Lord of hosts liveth, before whom I stand, I will surely shew myself unto him to day. So Obadiah went to meet Ahab, and told him: and Ahab went to meet Elijah.

1 Kings 18:1-16

The famine had raged for over three years (Luke 4:25 and James 5:17). Pastures and plants were affected. Water dried up. Food was scarce. Ahab was livid and had searched for Elijah throughout the land. Finally, the Bible says that after many days, God spoke to Elijah and gave him the next step. He told him to go and show himself again to wicked King Ahab.

Are you noticing the pattern? Elijah never moved from where he was until he received direction from God. Don't be in a hurry. Don't let people pressure you. Wait where you are until God speaks to you.

DON'T ACT UNTIL GOD SPEAKS

I remember years ago in one of our meetings in Latin America, I called my staff to my hotel room for our usual pre-crusade prayer meetings. As we began to pray, I felt a sense of urgency and we continued to intercede. Some of my staff were getting nervous, peeking at their watches, knowing they needed to be on the way to the stadium to train ushers and take care of other responsibilities. Still, I could not release them until God gave the word. Finally, God spoke. He told me not to take an offering in the meeting that night.

Now this was highly unusual as we always took an offering to cover the local expenses. But I told my associate, "Don't take an offering this evening." I didn't learn until later that there was a gang of men who had planned to disrupt the meeting that night. They had agreed that when the offering was collected, they would storm the platform, steal the money, and disrupt the meeting. The offering was their cue to act, but their cue never came.

What if I had yielded to the pressure of a schedule and ended our prayer meeting early? What if I had refused to listen to God and taken the offering as usual? Don't act until God gives direction. Remain where you are until it comes!

On another occasion in Mexico, Theresa and I left our hotel room for a meeting where some 25,000 Nationals had assembled for training. Coming out of the hotel elevator, God told me to return to the room and leave Theresa behind, which I did. As I exited the hotel, I was arrested by several burly policemen and taken to police headquarters for interrogation by Mexican officials who were opposed to the meeting. Theresa was able to continue on to the meeting, speak in my place, and lead intercession which resulted in my release later that day.

As an Elijah, knowing God's voice is vital to the success of your mission.

CHALLENGING OBADIAH

When God directed Elijah to return, he first encounters Obadiah, the King's governor, who is in search of any possible remaining pasture for the flocks. Obadiah had an important place of authority, next in rank to the king, and managed the palace and its affairs.

Obadiah is an enigma. His name means, "servant of my god," but Obadiah apparently served God behind the scenes up to this point. This great man secretly used his power for the protection of God's prophets. He hid 100 of them in caves, when the persecution was hot, and fed them with bread and water. Bread and water were now scarce commodities because of the famine, yet Obadiah somehow found a way to keep these men of God alive.

When Obadiah meets Elijah, he addresses him as "my lord," but Elijah tells him to go tell "his lord" (Ahab) that the prophet was back in town. Obadiah was a man who had achieved power, prestige, and position without endangering himself. He did good deeds behind the scenes and maintained a remote testimony for God rather than an open one. He lived within his comfort zone. It appears that God was his Savior, but not his lord, as the prophet's poignant comment drove home, "Go tell your lord."

Elijah challenged Obadiah to open action. He told him to go tell Ahab that he knew where Elijah was, but this was a request that carried a tremendous risk. Ahab might have thought Obadiah knew where Elijah was all along, and Obadiah was fearful:

> And he said, What have I sinned, that thou wouldest deliver thy servant into the hand of Ahab, to slay me? As the Lord thy God liveth, there is no nation or kingdom, whither my Lord hath not sent to seek thee: and when they said, He is not there; he took an oath of the kingdom and nation, that they found thee not.

1 Kings 18:9-10

Obadiah was fearful, but eventually he agreed to take the prophet's message to Ahab.

SECRET SERVICE CHRISTIANS

In these end times, the Church cannot be people of divided visions, loyalties, and affections. We cannot be "secret service" Christians, ignoring the evil around us and remaining in our comfort zones.

As an Elijah, God will use you to challenge people like Obadiah, those who are serving God in nominal ways, believers living in their comfort zones, those who are afraid to step out and bear God's message to an evil world. Like Obadiah, these people are basically good individuals and have a heart for God, but they need to be challenged to move into a new dimension of power and authority.

Like Elijah, you will challenge them to boldly proclaim the word of the Lord and, as they respond, the Spirit of the Lord will come upon them and catapult them to a new level in God. Under your mentoring, these "Obadiahs" have the potential to become Elishas—men and women to whom you can pass on the mantle of anointing and who will bear the message of God to a lost and dying world.

CHAPTER EIGHT

THE TROUBLER OF ISRAEL

A nd it came to pass, when Ahab saw Elijah, that Ahab said unto him, Art thou he that troubleth Israel? And he answered, I have not troubled Israel; but thou, and thy father's house, in that ye have forsaken the commandments of the Lord, and thou hast followed Baalim.

1 Kings 18:17-18

For more than three years, thanks to Elijah's prayer and prophecy, there had been no rain. As a result, there had been drought, hunger, starvation, and death. People were angry, and a lot of their anger was targeted on the prophet.

At last, Elijah and Ahab meet face to face. "Are you the one that troubles Israel?" snaps Ahab. The wicked king still refused to take responsibility for the results of his own sin. "Are you the one?" he accuses. People cannot change and negative circumstances cannot change until there is an acceptance of personal responsibility for sin.

Confrontation is not easy. Elijah's method with Obadiah had been compassionate and patient. With Ahab, his method is powerful and bold. Different personalities require different approaches. As an Elijah, you must discern, listen, and understand what to do in confrontational situations.

Elijah's new nickname was the "troubler of Israel" (1 Kings 18:17). The Hebrew verb "troubler" means "to disturb, stir up, and cause trouble." Whenever people disturb our comfort zones and challenge us, we often label them as troublemakers. Sometimes, however, we need to examine ourselves to see if we need to repent and change our ways.

As an Elijah, you will be called to challenge the status quo. You will speak out against sin and you will probably be shunned or criticized because of it. They may call you names. You may be falsely accused. Don't worry about it. Elijah was there before you. I've been there too!

Elijah had the boldness to confront Ahab because he knew he was an ambassador for the Lord. He knew the Lord was his helper and he didn't fear man (Hebrews 13:6). As David, he believed, *"The Lord is on my side; I will not fear: what can man do unto me"*(Psalm 118:6)?

GO TO THE ROOT CAUSE

Without hesitation, in the face of Ahab's accusations, Elijah went to the root cause of the problem. He declared, *"...I have not troubled Israel; but thou, and thy father's house, in that ye have forsaken the commandments of the Lord, and thou hast followed Baalim"* (1 Kings 18:18-18).

The root problems were rejecting God's commands and turning to idolatry. The effects were the famine. The problem was not the famine itself. The root problem is not addiction, it is what is at the root of addiction. It is not anger and bitterness, but what is at the root of anger and bitterness. Learn to confront the root causes instead of surface symptoms.

As an Elijah, you will minister to those who, like Ahab, are in the clutches of the enemy. They will rise up against you, as Ahab did Elijah, but you must be strong and confrontational in the power of the Lord. You cannot back down.

Elijah challenged Ahab to gather together all the people of Israel and the prophets of Baal. He said:

> *Now therefore send, and gather to me all Israel unto mount Carmel, and the prophets of Baal four hundred and fifty, and the prophets of the groves four hundred, which eat at Jezebel's table. So Ahab sent unto all the children of Israel, and gathered the prophets together unto mount Carmel.*

> 1 Kings 18:19-20

KNOW YOUR SOURCE OF AUTHORITY

You don't do something like this unless you know your source of authority. Seven sons of the priest learned this in New Testament times:

> *Then certain of the vagabond Jews, exorcists, took upon them to call over them which had evil spirits the name of the Lord Jesus, saying, We adjure you by Jesus whom Paul preacheth.And there were seven sons of one Sceva, a Jew, and chief of the priests, which did so. And the evil spirit answered and said, Jesus I know, and Paul I know; but who are ye? And the man in whom the evil spirit was leaped on*

them, and overcame them, and prevailed against them, so that they fled out of that house naked and wounded.

Acts 19:13-16

The power within you is greater than all of the power of the enemy, but it is only great if you know Jesus personally. You can't rely on the experience of others. You must have your own experience with God that takes you beyond the point of blessing into the realm of power.

Ahab complied, and brought the people and false prophets together at Mt. Carmel. So, here they stand on Mt. Carmel: Elijah, Ahab, the false prophets, and all of Israel.

CHAPTER NINE

LET THE FIRE FALL

*A*nd Elijah came unto all the people, and said, How long halt ye between two opinions? if the Lord be God, follow him: but if Baal, then follow him. And the people answered him not a word. Then said Elijah unto the people, I, even I only, remain a prophet of the Lord; but Baal's prophets are four hundred and fifty men. Let them therefore give us two bullocks; and let them choose one bullock for themselves, and cut it in pieces, and lay it on wood, and put no fire under: and I will dress the other bullock, and lay it on wood, and put no fire under: And call ye on the name of your gods, and I will call on the name of the Lord: and the God that answereth by fire, let him be God. And all the people answered and said, It is well spoken. And Elijah said unto the prophets of Baal, Choose you one bullock for yourselves, and dress it first; for ye are many; and call on the name of your gods, but put no fire under. And they took the bullock which was given them, and they dressed it, and called on the name of Baal from morning even until noon, saying, O Baal, hear us. But there was no voice, nor any that answered. And they leaped upon the altar which was made. And it came to pass at noon, that Elijah mocked them, and said, Cry aloud: for he is a god; either he is talking, or he is pursuing, or he is in a journey, or peradventure he sleepeth, and must be awaked. And they cried aloud, and cut themselves after their manner with knives and lancets, till the blood gushed out upon them. And it came to pass, when midday was past, and they prophesied until the time of the offering of the evening sacrifice, that there was neither voice, nor any to answer, nor any that regarded. And Elijah said unto all the people, Come near unto me. And all the people came near unto him. And he repaired the altar of the Lord that was broken down. And Elijah took twelve stones, according to the number of the tribes of the sons of Jacob, unto whom the word of the Lord came, saying, Israel shall be thy name: And with the stones he built an altar in the name of the Lord: and he made a trench about the altar, as great as would contain two measures of seed. And he put the wood in order, and cut the bullock in pieces, and laid him on the wood, and said, Fill four barrels with water, and pour it on the burnt sacrifice, and on the wood. And he said, Do it the second time. And they did it the second time. And he said, Do it the third time. And they did it the third time. And the *water ran round about the altar; and he filled the trench also with water. And it came to pass at the time of the offering of the evening sacrifice, that Elijah the prophet came near, and said, Lord God of Abraham, Isaac, and of Israel, let it be known this day that thou art God in Israel, and that I am thy servant, and that I have done all these things at thy word. Hear me, O Lord, hear me, that this people may know that thou art the Lord God, and that thou hast turned their heart back again. Then the fire of the Lord fell, and consumed the burnt sacrifice, and the wood, and the stones, and the dust, and licked up the water that was in the trench. And when all the people saw it, they fell on their faces: and they said, The Lord, he is the God; the Lord, he is the God. And Elijah said unto them, Take the prophets of Baal; let not one of them escape. And they took them: and Elijah brought them down to the brook Kishon, and slew them there.*

1 Kings 18:21-30

Elijah, wicked King Ahab, the prophets of Baal, and all of Israel had assembled on Mt. Carmel.

In a thunderous voice, the prophet asked, *"How long halt ye between two opinions? if the Lord be God, follow him: but if Baal, then follow him. And the people answered him not a word"* (1 Kings 18:21).

Hesitation is double-mindedness. The term "double-minded" refers to the unsteadiness of a person because of indecision. Halting between two opinions is like limping on two unequal legs or a bird flitting from branch to branch. Many people live lives of duplicity today. They go to church on Sunday, but where are they on Saturday night?

If you are to minister in the spirit and power of Elijah, you must be single-minded. Jesus said: *"...The light of the body is the eye: therefore when thine eye is single , thy whole body also is full of light; but when thine eye is evil, thy body also is full of darkness"* (Luke 11:34).

Today we hear a lot about religious tolerance and how there are "many ways to God." But the Bible declares there is only one way to God:

For there is one God, and one mediator between God and men, the man Christ Jesus; Who gave himself a ransom for all, to be testified in due time.

1 Timothy 2:5-6

There are only two spiritual paths, one which leads to God and results in blessing, the other leads to death and destruction.

Enter ye in at the strait gate: for wide is the gate, and broad is the way, that leadeth to destruction, and many there be which go in thereat: Because strait is the gate, and narrow is the way, which leadeth unto life, and few there be that find it.

Matthew 7:13-14

God spoke through Malachi:

Behold, I will send you, Elijah the prophet, before the coming of the great and dreadful day of the Lord. And he will turn the hearts of the fathers to the children, and the hearts of the children to their fathers, lest I come and strike the earth with a curse.

Malachi 4:5-6

One of the major functions of the prophetic ministry in this hour will be to confront the corrupt religious establishment as Elijah did. You will be used by God to expose sin, bring forth truth that has been cast aside, and open the eyes of those who have been blinded by man's traditions and doctrines.

Under this prophetic mantle, those who minister in the spirit and power of Elijah will call the Church to repentance. God will give them prophetic visions and reveal existing conditions within people, churches, cities, and nations that are contrary to the Word and that are bringing destruction. As people respond to the Word of the Lord, repent, and turn away from those things that are grieving His Spirit and that are contrary to His Word, God will release strength, healing, and will deliver them from every bondage of the enemy.

God will use these end-time ministers with the Elijah anointing to warn of His judgments that are coming upon this world. Through their prophetic ministry, believers will be strengthened and prepared to stand against the powers of darkness.

THE CHALLENGE ON CARMEL

There on Mt. Carmel, Elijah told the people:

...Baal's prophets are four hundred and fifty men. Let them therefore

give us two bullocks; and let them choose one bullock for themselves,
and cut it in pieces, and lay it on wood, and put no fire under: and
I will dress the other bullock, and lay it on wood, and put no fire
under: And call ye on the name of your gods, and I will call on the
name of the Lord: and the God that answereth by fire, let him be
God. And all the people answered and said, It is well spoken.

1 Kings 18:22- 25

Elijah told the prophets of Baal to select a bullock, prepare it, put it on an altar, but kindle no fire under it. He would do the same. The sacrifice that was consumed by fire would confirm the true God. The prophets of Baal obeyed, built an altar, and beseeched their gods from morning to evening, with no results. No voice. No one answered. No fire fell. They leaped on the altar, cried aloud, and even cut themselves with knives. Still, no response. Baal was worshiped as the "Lord of the Fire," and some adherents even passed their children through fire as an act of worship (2 Kings 16:3). Mt. Carmel was also a sacred place where they believed the power of Baal was dominant. This is why it was so significant that no fire fell when Baal was entreated.

REBUILDING THE ALTAR

Finally, around the time of the evening sacrifice, Elijah said to the people:

And Elijah said unto all the people, Come near unto me. And all the
people came near unto him. And he repaired the altar of the Lord
that was broken down. And Elijah took twelve stones, according to
the number of the tribes of the sons of Jacob, unto whom the word of
the Lord came, saying, Israel shall be thy name: And with the stones
he built an altar in the name of the Lord: and he made a trench
about the altar, as great as would contain two measures of seed.
And he put the wood in order, and cut the bullock in pieces, and laid
him on the wood, and said, Fill four barrels with water, and pour
it on the burnt sacrifice, and on the wood. And he said, Do it the
second time. And they did it the second time. And he said, Do it the
third time. And they did it the third time. And the water ran round
about the altar; and he filled the trench also with water.

1 Kings 18:30-35

The prophets of Baal built their own altar, but Elijah rebuilt the altar of

the Lord which had been broken down. The fire of God will not fall on our man-made altars. Elijah used 12 stones to rebuild the altar, symbolizing the number of the tribes of Israel and demonstrating that God had never accepted their division (Joshua 4:8). Division always hinders what God wants to do in your life and ministry.

The altar of God is a place of sacrifice, true worship, full surrender, and death to self. We are exhorted by Paul to present our bodies as a *"...living sacrifice holy, acceptable unto God"* (Romans 12:1). This is not the exception, but rather our *"reasonable service."* It is required of us.

Is it possible that the altar of the Lord in our lives and churches has been torn down through sin, unholy desires, worldliness, selfishness, disobedience, and our unwillingness to sacrifice our lives for the sake of the Gospel? Is it possible that through lack of dedication of our lives, talents, and finances to God, the altar of the Lord has been torn down?

We must not allow the altars in our churches, ministries, and Christian organizations to become polluted by impure motives, selfish ambitions, or sensual and worldly desires. Just as Elijah confronted the apostate nation of Israel and the false religious system, God will use those with the Elijah anointing to confront the backslidden Church today.

God is calling for restoration of His altar corporately in His Church as well as individually. Elijah used twelve stones to rebuild the altar of God on Mt. Carmel and I believe there are twelve things that must be restored to the Church in rebuilding the altar of God:

1. Holiness instead of worldliness.
2. The fear of the Lord instead of fear of man.
3. A total dependence upon God instead of leaning to the arm of the flesh.
4. True worship instead of entertainment.
5. Death to self instead of self-centeredness.
6. Burden and love for the unsaved instead of apathy.
7. Spiritual hunger instead of complacency.
8. True dedication and consecration to God instead of half-heartedness.
9. One hundred percent obedience instead of disobedience.
10. Hatred for sin instead of compromise.
11. Humility instead of pride and self-exaltation.
12. Unselfishness instead of selfishness.

If we want the fire of God to fall on our lives and congregations again, then the altar of God must be rebuilt!

GET READY – THE FIRE IS FALLING!

After rebuilding the altar, Elijah dug a trench around the altar, stacked the wood, and placed the bullock on the altar. Then he asked that four barrels of water be poured over the sacrifice and the wood. He asked that this be repeated two more times. A total of 12 barrels of water saturated the sacrifice and the altar. Elijah prepared for the move of God. You must prepare the altar of your heart for the fire of God. You must rebuild the altars that have been broken down. You must get ready for God to move!

> And it came to pass at the time of the offering of the evening sacrifice, that Elijah the prophet came near, and said, Lord God of Abraham, Isaac, and of Israel, let it be known this day that thou art God in Israel, and that I am thy servant, and that I have done all these things at thy word. Hear me, O Lord, hear me, that this people may know that thou art the Lord God, and that thou hast turned their heart back again. Then the fire of the Lord fell, and consumed the burnt sacrifice, and the wood, and the stones, and the dust, and licked up the water that was in the trench. And when all the people saw it, they fell on their faces: and they said, The Lord, he is the God; the Lord, he is the God. And Elijah said unto them, Take the prophets of Baal; let not one of them escape. And they took them: and Elijah brought them down to the brook Kishon, and slew them there.

1 Kings 18:36-40

At the time of the evening sacrifice, Elijah called on God and declared,

> Lord God of Abraham, Isaac, and of Israel, let it be known this day that thou art God in Israel, and that I am thy servant, and that I have done all these things at thy word. Hear me, O Lord, hear me, that this people may know that thou art the Lord God, and that thou hast turned their heart back again.

1 Kings 18:36-37

Let us examine the contents of his brief, but powerful prayer:

"Let it be known that Thou art God in Israel": People need to see that there is a true God.

"That I am Thy servant": Miracles verify both the Word of God and the messenger of God. Be clear on where you stand. You are not people-controlled. You are God-controlled. You are His servant.

"That I have done all these things at Thy Word": Your life and ministry, all you do, is to be ordered by the Word, not by emotions or the ideas of others. Don't do your thing and then ask God to bless it. Do God's thing.

"That Thou hast turned their heart back again": Elijah sought no credit for what was about to happen. It was God who would turn their hearts. The demonstration of God's miracle-working power is always for the purpose of confirming that He is God and turning the hearts of people back to Him. That is why you should always preach the greatest miracle of salvation when you conduct healing and deliverance services. Always remember that God is a God of purpose, design, and objectivity. He has divine purpose for everything He does and all He commands you to do.

God does not hear us for our flowery words or our long appeals. It is not the length of our prayers that makes them powerful, but whether or not they are aligned with the will of God. When you pray in the name of Jesus, in the will of God, for the purposes of God, then every prayer you pray will be answered every time. You will know no defeat in prayer.

LET THE FIRE FALL

God heard Elijah's prayer and the fire from God fell and the sacrifice, the wood, the stones, the dust, and the water were consumed. When the people saw it, they fell on their faces and declared, *"...The Lord, he is God; the Lord, he is God"* (1 Kings 18:39).

Then Elijah told them to slay all the prophets of Baal and they complied.

The key to the release of God's power through Elijah's prayers was not because of a formula he followed. It was not because of the words he spoke. It was because of his relationship with God.

Elijah was a man with a nature that was subject to the same feelings, passions, and desires you and I have:

Elijah was a human being with a nature such as we have [with feelings, affections and a constitution like ours]; and he prayed earnestly for it not to rain, and no rain fell on the earth for three

*years and six months. And [then] he prayed again and the heavens
supplied rain and the land produced its crops [as usual].*

James 5:17-18 AMP

We will witness Elijah's humanness when we study 1 Kings 19, where
his bout with depression is recorded.

Elijah was not special. God has planned for you to have this same
power through prayer. James said, *"And the prayer of faith shall save the
sick…"* (James 5:15). He said, *"The earnest, (heartfelt, continued) prayer
of a righteous man makes tremendous power available [dynamic in its
working]"* (James 5:16, AMP). The Greek word for *"availeth"*, is used in this
passage in the King James version of the Bible, and it is a very significant
word. It basically means "to be strong," "to have power or force," and "to
exercise power." The prayer of a righteous man avails much. Definite and
determined prayer exerts great power in its manifestation. It achieves great
things.

There are many Christians who pray, but they are only speaking empty
words. They have not developed an intimate relationship with God where
they truly know Him and know He will hear and do all He has promised.
Without this intimate relationship there can be no real power.

Healing of chronic illnesses and terminal sicknesses and diseases,
salvation of sinners, financial breakthroughs, open doors for the Gospel,
an end-time outpouring of God's Spirit, and a worldwide harvest of souls
will come as God's people enter into a new dimension of prayer and begin
to pray Holy Spirit energized, effectual, fervent prayers. As an Elijah, you
must learn this. When you are standing in front of an entire nation, you
better know how to pray! Those nursery prayers just won't do.

Years ago, in a place called Yosemite National Park in California, there
was a spectacular ritual conducted nightly during tourist season. A huge
bonfire was built at the top of Yosemite Falls, one of the tallest waterfalls in
the world. As the people sat far below, the park ranger would shout, "Let
the fire fall!" The bonfire would be pushed over the ledge and a spectacular
"water fall" of liquid fire would descend.

Our response is, "Do it again, Lord!" As You did on Mt. Carmel–let
the fire fall upon your people! We seek the double-portion anointing. Let a
new, supernatural mantle, infused with the fire of God, descend upon us.

CHAPTER TEN

IT'S BEGINNING TO RAIN

*A*nd Elijah said unto Ahab, Get thee up, eat and drink; for there
*is a sound of abundance of rain. So Ahab went up to eat and to
drink. And Elijah went up to the top of Carmel; and he cast himself
down upon the earth, and put his face between his knees, And said
to his servant, Go up now, look toward the sea. And he went up,
and looked, and said, There is nothing. And he said, Go again seven
times. And it came to pass at the seventh time, that he said, Behold,
there ariseth a little cloud out of the sea, like a man's hand. And he
said, Go up, say unto Ahab, Prepare thy chariot, and get thee down,
that the rain stop thee not. And it came to pass in the mean while,
that the heaven was black with clouds and wind, and there was a
great rain. And Ahab rode, and went to Jezreel. And the hand of the
Lord was on Elijah; and he girded up his loins, and ran before Ahab
to the entrance of Jezreel.*

1 Kings 18:41:46

After the miraculous demonstration of the fire of God, Elijah declared
to Ahab, "You better get on the road home because I hear the sound of an
abundance of rain!"

Can you imagine the problems the extended drought had created? Just
visualize some of the scenes of starvation in modern-day Africa and you will
get the picture. Now, without a cloud in the sky, Elijah declared that he
heard the sound of an abundant rain. He spoke the miracle into existence
before he received the visible manifestation. That is the spirit of the Elijah
generation–men and women who call those things which are not as though
they were and who against hope, believe in hope (Romans 4:17-18).

Ahab started home and Elijah retreated to Mt. Carmel to pray for rain.
You will remember that Elijah had prayed once, and the rains ceased. He
had prayed once, and the fire fell. But this time, Elijah had to persevere in
prayer.

Elijah prayed, then sent his servant to check the skies. No clouds. He
prayed again and sent his servant to check again. No clouds. Six times
this was repeated, but on the seventh time, the servant reported "There is a

small cloud...about the size of a man's hand."

DON'T GIVE UP

In Luke 18, Jesus told a parable to illustrate that His followers should pray and not faint (lose heart and give up). Jesus used the example of a widow to emphasize a deep level of need. A widow at that time often had no family or other resources upon which they could depend. With no one to turn to for help, the widow in this parable went to an unjust judge and pleaded her case saying, "...*Avenge me of my adversary*" (Luke 18:3).

The widow's cries fell on deaf ears, however. The unjust judge refused to do anything to help her (Luke 18:4) We do not know how much time passed, but the widow did not give up. She kept persevering with shameless persistence that did not stop until the unjust judge helped her.

The unjust judge, seeing that she was not going to give up and go away, said to himself, "...*Even though I don't fear God or care about men, yet because this widow keeps bothering me, I will see that she gets justice, so that she won't eventually wear me out with her coming*" (Luke 18:4, NIV).

The widow pressed her way in and broke through all resistance by her perseverance. She received what she asked and her need was met.

In this parable, Jesus was teaching us to be like this widow, to persevere in prayer until we have an answer. Our judge is not unjust. Come to God with total dependence upon Him, knowing He has bound Himself by His Word to answer your prayers. Pray with this persistence until the answer comes.

If the unjust judge responded to the persistent cries of the widow who he didn't know and didn't really care about, how much more will God respond to His beloved children who persistently cry out to Him (Luke 18:6-7).

When we pray, if we do not receive the answer the first time, we should go back the second time. If we do not receive an answer the third, fourth, or even the hundredth time, we are to persevere until we receive it. This is not lack of faith. This is perseverance, and Jesus taught and greatly valued this kind of faith.

ELIJAH'S HOUR OF POWER

Elijah persevered in prayer until the rain began to fall. As we look at incidents like these in Elijah's life, we like to think that he is someone special and not like us. But the Bible declares:

> *Elias was a man subject to like passions as we are, and he prayed earnestly that it might not rain: and it rained not on the earth by the space of three years and six months. And he prayed again, and the heaven gave rain, and the earth brought forth her fruit.*

James 5:17-18

Elijah was a man subject to similar passions and emotions. He was only human, as we will see in the next chapter. But all through Scripture, God takes ordinary people and makes them extraordinary. He is not looking at what you are, but He is seeing you as you will be when you receive the mantle of the double-portion anointing and begin to minister in the spirit and power of Elijah.

This was Elijah's hour of power. The rain began to fall, and Elijah hiked up his robes and outran Ahab's chariot. But beware: The hour of power often precedes the hour of peril.

CHAPTER ELEVEN

COMING OUT OF THE CAVE

And Ahab told Jezebel all that Elijah had done, and withal how he had slain all the prophets with the sword. Then Jezebel sent a messenger unto Elijah, saying, So let the gods do to me, and more also, if I make not thy life as the life of one of them by to morrow about this time. And when he saw that, he arose, and went for his life, and came to Beer-sheba, which belongeth to Judah, and left his servant there. But he himself went a day's journey into the wilderness, and came and sat down under a juniper tree: and he requested for himself that he might die; and said, It is enough; now, O Lord, take away my life; for I am not better than my fathers. And as he lay and slept under a juniper tree, behold, then an angel touched him, and said unto him, Arise and eat. And he looked, and, behold, there was a cake baken on the coals, and a cruse of water at his head. And he did eat and drink, and laid him down again. And the angel of the Lord came again the second time, and touched him, and said, Arise and eat; because the journey is too great for thee. And he arose, and did eat and drink, and went in the strength of that meat forty days and forty nights unto Horeb the mount of God. And he came thither unto a cave, and lodged there; and, behold, the word of the Lord came to him, and he said unto him, What doest thou here, Elijah? And he said, I have been very jealous for the Lord God of hosts: for the children of Israel have forsaken thy covenant, thrown down thine altars, and slain thy prophets with the sword; and I, even I only, am left; and they seek my life, to take it away. And he said, Go forth, and stand upon the mount before the Lord. And, behold, the Lord passed by, and a great and strong wind rent the mountains, and brake in pieces the rocks before the Lord; but the Lord was not in the wind: and after the wind an earthquake; but the Lord was not in the earthquake: And after the earthquake a fire; but the Lord was not in the fire: and after the fire a still small voice. And it was so, when Elijah heard it, that he wrapped his face in his mantle, and went out, and stood in the entering in of the cave. And, behold, there came a voice unto him, and said, What doest thou here, Elijah? And he said, I have been very jealous for the Lord God of hosts: because the children of Israel have forsaken thy covenant, thrown down thine altars, and slain thy prophets with the sword; and I, even I only, am left; and they seek my life, to take it away.

And the Lord said unto him, Go, return on thy way to the wilderness of Damascus: and when thou comest, anoint Hazael to be king over Syria: And Jehu the son of Nimshi shalt thou anoint to be king over Israel: and Elisha the son of Shaphat of Abel-meholah shalt thou anoint to be prophet in thy room. And it shall come to pass, that him that escapeth the sword of Hazael shall Jehu slay: and him that escapeth from the sword of Jehu shall Elisha slay. Yet I have left me seven thousand in Israel, all the knees which have not bowed unto Baal, and every mouth which hath not kissed him.

1 Kings 19:1-18

In 1 Kings 18, we witness Elijah during his hour of power. But in 1 Kings 19, we find God's man of faith and power in trouble. After the dramatic incident on Mt. Carmel, Elijah was put on the King's hit list, so he fled for his life:

And when he saw that, he arose, and went for his life, and came to Beer-sheba, which belongeth to Judah, and left his servant there. But he himself went a day's journey into the wilderness, and came and sat down under a juniper tree: and he requested for himself that he might die; and said, It is enough; now, O Lord, take away my life; for I am not better than my fathers.

1 Kings 19:3-4

Think of all Elijah had seen: The drought in answer to his prophetic prayer; supernatural provision at Cherith and in the widow's household; the raising of the widow's son from the dead; the fire of God falling on Mount Carmel; the end of the drought with a deluge of rain; and supernatural strength to outrun a chariot. But you cannot live on past victories. They simply will not sustain you.

Be careful after great victories, for times of testing often follow. David fell into sin at the height of his military career when he had known no defeats. Jonah fell into despondency after one of the greatest revivals in history–the whole city repented. Peter denied Christ after his powerful declaration of loyalty. And Elijah fell into fear and discouragement after witnessing the fire of God fall from Heaven.

I believe the reason God included this account in Scripture is so we would know that God uses men and women–just like you and me–despite their emotions and passions. He included this account not so we could use it as a reason for defeat, but so we could grasp the strategies for victory that are revealed in this story.

ELIJAH'S PROBLEMS

One problem that plunged Elijah into desperation was that he became preoccupied with his own survival. His focus was no longer on God, but it was on self. The minute you get your eyes off God and onto self, you are in trouble. In difficult times, you must remember that it is not about you. It is about God and His purposes.

Another problem was fear. Faith energies, but fear paralyzes. When you begin to move in fear, you lose your energy and enthusiasm for God's work. If you don't deal with fear, you will end up like Elijah–hiding in the wilderness and retreating to a cave.

Elijah was also physically tired and emotionally spent from dealing with the evils of his time. Elijah fled to the wilderness, sat down under a juniper tree in the wilderness, and poured out his pain to God. A juniper is a desert shrub which can grow up to 10 feet high, but gives poor protection from the hot desert sun. Every "juniper tree" of this world provides poor protection in times of trouble. Only God provides adequate shelter. David declared:

> *For thou hast been a shelter for me, and a strong tower from the enemy. I will abide in thy tabernacle for ever: I will trust in the covert of thy wings. Selah.*

> Psalm 61:34

Siting under the straggly tree, Elijah began to pray. Somehow, we have the idea that our prayers should always be polite and pious. Nice words don't grab God's attention, but heartfelt, honest cries for help do. God knows what is in your heart. He knows when you feel angry or depressed. He knows when you are tired and when you feel abandoned. When you have had enough of the circumstances of life, come to God in prayer and tell Him about it. He won't reject you. Share your true feelings. Linger in His presence.

Elijah was so discouraged that he wanted to die. He had just had it! It was enough! Elijah poured out his heart to God and then fell asleep, probably from exhaustion. While he slept, an angel was dispatched to minister to him:

> *And as he lay and slept under a juniper tree, behold, then an angel touched him, and said unto him, Arise and eat. And he looked, and,*

behold, there was a cake baken on the coals, and a cruse of water at his head. And he did eat and drink, and laid him down again. And the angel of the Lord came again the second time, and touched him, and said, Arise and eat; because the journey is too great for thee. And he arose, and did eat and drink, and went in the strength of that meat forty days and forty nights unto Horeb the mount of God.

1 Kings 19:5-8

God heard Elijah's prayer and sent an angel to prepare food and water, telling him that the journey was too great for him. You may think you can make it on your own, but you can't. You need divine provision. When the journey grows too great for you, take time to get in the presence, of God. Talk to Him. Take time to rest and eat properly, because, *"It is vain for you to rise up early, to sit up late, to eat the bread of sorrows: for so he giveth his beloved sleep"* (Psalm 127:2).

Sometimes, even an Elijah needs simple rest and refreshment. Feast on the food and water of the Word of God, and like Elijah, you will be able to journey onward with supernatural strength.

Renewed by rest and God's tender care, Elijah went in the strength of the food for 40 days and nights until he arrived at Mt. Horeb. Actually, from where Elijah began, it is not a 40-day journey from Beer-Sheba to Mt. Horeb. Elijah was wandering, just as the children of Israel had when they were in the desert. Whether it be 40 years or 40 days, we are prone to prolong our wilderness trek in pursuit of our own plans and solutions.

WHY ARE YOU HERE?

Mt. Horeb is where Moses met with God and received the ten commandments and the revelations about the tabernacle and priesthood. It was a sacred place where God had manifested Himself in a cloud of glory. It was here that Elijah went and hid himself in a cave. After all, at least 100 other prophets were hiding in caves for self-preservation.

He hid himself, but he was not hidden from God. The Lord came and asked him, "What are you doing here?" Not that God didn't know, but He asked for the same reason He questioned Adam and Eve in the Garden, "Where art thou?" He wanted Elijah to face his true condition.

And he came thither unto a cave, and lodged there; and, behold, the
word of the Lord came to him, and he said unto him, What doest
thou here, Elijah? And he said, I have been very jealous for the Lord
God of hosts: for the children of Israel have forsaken thy covenant,
thrown down thine altars, and slain thy prophets with the sword;
and I, even I only, am left; and they seek my life, to take it away.

1 Kings 19:9-10

Elijah was deceived into thinking he was the only one left who was serving God. He was depressed and oppressed by the enemy and he was fearful.

Satan has seven major strategies that he will employ to try to defeat your mission:

- The strategy of depression.
- The strategy of oppression.
- The strategy of delusion
- The strategy of deception.
- The strategy of obsession.
- The strategy of fear.
- The strategy of possession.

These problems are universal and Satan tries to use them to hinder your calling and keep you from your destiny. Which ever strategy he uses, and whatever the reason you are in any of these cycles of defeat, God wants you to face your true condition. Why are you here? His word to you is:

Arise [from the depression and prostration in which circumstances
have kept you–rise to a new life]! Shine (be radiant with the glory
of the Lord), for your light has come and the glory of the Lord has
risen upon you!

Isaiah 60:1 AMP

As you minister in the spirit and power of Elijah, you will have great mountaintop victories. You will witness great miracles. But there will be times when you feel all alone, and that is how Elijah felt in this account. When God confronted him, Elijah felt like he was the only one standing against the evil of his times. Notice his focus on self: *"I, even I only, am left; and they seek my life..."*

God called Elijah out of the cave and told him to go stand on the mountain:

And he said, Go forth, and stand upon the mount before the Lord. And, behold, the Lord passed by, and a great and strong wind rent the mountains, and brake in pieces the rocks before the Lord; but the Lord was not in the wind: and after the wind an earthquake; but the Lord was not in the earthquake: And after the earthquake a fire; but the Lord was not in the fire: and after the fire a still small voice. And it was so, when Elijah heard it, that he wrapped his face in his mantle, and went out, and stood in the entering in of the cave. And, behold, there came a voice unto him, and said, What doest thou here, Elijah? And he said, I have been very jealous for the Lord God of hosts: because the children of Israel have forsaken thy covenant, thrown down thine altars, and slain thy prophets with the sword; and I, even I only, am left; and they seek my life, to take it away

1 Kings 19:11-14

As Elijah stood on the mountain, the Lord passed by and a strong wind tore the mountainside, so great that it shattered rocks. Spectacular! But the Lord was not in the wind. Then there was a tremendous earthquake, but again–the Lord was not in it. Then came a fire...this must be God! After all, fire fell from Heaven on Mt. Carmel! But this time, God was not in the fire. You can't put God in a mold and expect Him to manifest Himself the same way every time.

THE STILL SMALL VOICE

Suddenly, there came the "still, small voice" of God. The route back from discouragement and despair is not by running, hiding, or waiting for miraculous demonstrations. It is to once again hear the still small voice of God.

Again, God asks Elijah, "What are you doing here?" He allows Elijah to vent his frustrations, then God speaks:

And the Lord said unto him, Go, return on thy way to the wilderness of Damascus: and when thou comest, anoint Hazael to be king over Syria: And Jehu the son of Nimshi shalt thou anoint to be king over Israel: and Elisha the son of Shaphat of Abel-meholah shalt thou anoint to be prophet in thy room. And it shall come to pass, that him that escapeth the sword of Hazael shall Jehu slay: and him that escapeth from the sword of Jehu shall Elisha slay. Yet I have left me seven thousand in Israel, all the knees which have not bowed unto

Baal, and every mouth which hath not kissed him.

1 Kings 19:15-18

God doesn't leave us on the mountain top of victory. He sends us back to the valleys of this world amidst human misery and need to accomplish His purposes. God tells Elijah to return and...

...go by the way to the wilderness of Damascus.
...anoint Hazael to be king over Syria.
...anoint Jehu, the son of Nimshi, to be king over Israel.
...anoint Elisha, the son of Shaphat of Abel-meholah, to be a
    prophet in his place.

God gave Elijah specific directions. He gave him new goals and objectives. Elijah's work was not complete just because of a bout with discouragement. He still had prophetic purpose to fulfill, and most importantly, he would raise up a successor. He would anoint Elisha to receive the mantle of his ministry.

"Oh, and by the way," the Lord mentioned. "You are not alone, even though you feel that way. I have 7,000 others in Israel who have not bowed to Baal."

You are not alone. God always has a people!
The Apostle Paul declared:

I say then, Hath God cast away his people? God forbid. For I also am an Israelite, of the seed of Abraham, of the tribe of Benjamin. God hath not cast away his people which he foreknew. Wot ye not what the scripture saith of Elias? how he maketh intercession to God against Israel, saying, Lord, they have killed thy prophets, and digged down thine altars; and I am left alone, and they seek my life. But what saith the answer of God unto him? I have reserved to myself seven thousand men, who have not bowed the knee to the image of Baal. Even so then at this present time also there is a remnant according to the election of grace. And if by grace, then is it no more of works: otherwise grace is no more grace. But if it be of works, then is it no more grace: otherwise work is no more work.

Romans 11:1-6

If you are truly ministering in the spirit and power of Elijah, you will have times of discouragement, as he did. The reason some people never get discouraged is because they are like the 100 prophets of Elijah's time that were hiding in caves. They aren't out on the front lines. They never leave their comfort zones.

COME OUT OF THE CAVE

A "cave" is anything which limits you spiritually. You may be hiding in the "cave" of limited resources, negative circumstances, bad relationships, lost dreams, or discouragement. If you are to fulfill your destiny, you must come out of the cave like Elijah did and embrace the plan of God.

God wants you to learn to be strong in Him. He wants you to be tough in difficult times. The word "tough" means" having the quality of being strong or firm in texture, but flexible and not brittle; yielding to for force without breaking; capable of resisting great strain without coming apart."

God called Elijah out of his cave. God called David out of the cave where he was hiding. He called Daniel out of the lion's den and the Hebrew men out of the fiery furnace. He supernaturally delivered Joseph, Peter, Paul, and Silas out of prison He took the Prophet Jeremiah out of the pit. He called Lazarus out of the tomb of death.

And now, it is time for YOU to come out. It is time for you to come forth in the spirit and power of Elijah! Leave your tomb mentality behind you. Don't look to the circumstances of your tomb.

Lazarus had been in the tomb so long he was stinking! Anything that keeps you bound in a tomb of despair, bondage, or defeat stinks! Jesus is coming to your tomb and, like He did for Elijah, He is calling you forth to new vision and purpose.

In the early years of my ministry, God gave a prophetic declaration that has helped me through difficult times. The next time you encounter despair, I encourage you to embrace these words:

God said:

Don't look to the bigness of your need. Look to the bigness of your God. Your circumstances are hindrances in seeing my abilities...If you keep your eyes on your circumstances the devil will use your circumstances to defeat you and accuse the Word of God ...the

written and the Living Word. Your victory is in keeping your eyes on the bigness of your God and His ability. He has promised to take you step, by step, by step ...not all at once, but step by step and each step will be a miracle!

CHAPTER TWELVE

THE MANTLE

In 1 Kings 19, we meet a chosen vessel named Elisha who is to become the protégé of the Prophet Elijah. The name Elisha means "My God is salvation," and it is representative of the message Elisha would bear to the nation.

> *So he departed thence, and found Elisha the son of Shaphat, who was plowing with twelve yoke of oxen before him, and he with the twelfth: and Elijah passed by him, and cast his mantle upon him. And he left the oxen, and ran after Elijah, and said, Let me, I pray thee, kiss my father and my mother, and then I will follow thee. And he said unto him, Go back again: for what have I done to thee? And he returned back from him, and took a yoke of oxen, and slew them, and boiled their flesh with the instruments of the oxen, and gave unto the people, and they did eat. Then he arose, and went after Elijah, and ministered unto him.*

1 Kings 19:19-21

When we first meet Elisha, we find that he wasn't sitting around waiting to be called into ministry. Elisha was working on the family farm. He probably came from a wealthy family, because plowing with so many oxen represented being in the upper class. Although Elisha belonged to a wealthy family, he was not irresponsible or lazy. He was hard at work in the field with the rest of the workers.

This is exactly the kind of character God chooses for position in His Kingdom. God calls busy men and women–not the lazy and slothful. He knows you are already busy, but He wants you to be willing to lay aside your plans for His purposes. The Elijahs that God is raising up to receive and pass on this anointing will often be busy people. They will have important jobs, ministries, families, and lands. But as the mantle of this anointing is placed upon their shoulders, they will leave it all to follow the call.

God called Moses in the midst of tending a flock. He called Matthew at the tax office. He called Peter, James, and John from their thriving fishing enterprise. Like these men, this anointing that God wants to place upon your life will change your plans, purpose, and destiny.

As we saw in the case of Elijah, there is not much revealed about Elisha's background or training. He hadn't been to prophet's school. He was a farmer. God is not interested in your ability as much as He is in your availability, and Elisha was available.

One day, in the midst of Elisha's routine duties, Elijah walked by the field and threw his mantle over him. The most dramatic moves of God often come right in the middle of the normal routines of life. Don't be so busy or exhausted by your routine that you ignore the significance of what is happening. Don't be so set in your own plans and purposes that you miss the call ("I must finish plowing this field first.").

When the mantle of Elijah descended upon his shoulders, there was something so powerful, so tremendous about it that Elisha immediately left his family, his farm, and his future. He killed the oxen with which he had been plowing, closing the door to any temptation to return to the old life. These are the people who, in the plan of God, become the ones who achieve great things for the Kingdom. When God speaks, there is no debate. They don't ask for a career path. There is no discussion. They simply respond in obedience, step out into the unknown to do God's will, and they never look back.

Elijah made it clear that the call was from God, not from him: *"And he said unto him, Go back again: for what have I done to thee?"* (1 Kings 19:20). The Elishas that are called to come under this anointing must realize it is not a call emanating from a man. It is not a mandate from Morris Cerullo. It is a supernatural call from Almighty God.

THE MANTLE UPON ELIJAH

What was it about this mantle that Elijah cast over Elisha that made him immediately forsake all for the call? We must grasp this revelation, for it is vital in recruiting Elishas to receive the double-portion anointing.

The word "mantle," as used in this passage, means "covered with a covering." Elijah's mantle was more than just a piece of cloth. It very possibly was the traditional prayer shawl worn by Hebrew men. Most important, this mantle was a divine token that was symbolic of three powerful spiritual truths:

1.   **It represented divine intimacy:** The first mention we have of Elijah's mantle is in 1 Kings 19:13 when Elijah fled to Mt. Horeb, tired and discouraged from his conflicts with Ahab, Jezebel, and the evil prophets of

Baal. It was here that God spoke to Elijah in a still, small voice and comforted him...

> *And it was so, when Elijah heard it, that he wrapped his face in his mantle, and went out, and stood in the entering in of the cave. And, behold, there came a voice unto him, and said, What doest thou here, Elijah?*

1 Kings 19:13

Elijah wrapped himself in his mantle while he communed with Almighty God and it became a symbol of intimate relationship with his Master. You cannot minister in the spirit and power of Elijah without an intimate relationship with God developed in the inner chamber, alone with God in prayer, study, and meditation. You must be wrapped in intimacy with God the Father.

2. It represented a supernatural calling: The second mention of Elijah's mantle is found in the account we are presently studying, when it is cast over Elisha:

> *So he (Elijah) departed thence, and found Elisha the son of Shaphat, who was plowing with twelve yoke of oxen before him, and he with the twelfth: and Elijah passed by him, and cast his mantle upon him.*

1 Kings 19:19

There was something so powerful invested in this mantle that when Elijah threw it across Elisha's shoulders, it caused him to leave life as he knew it and follow the prophet without reservation. No words were exchanged. No long debate about the pros and cons of responding. A supernatural call, an immediate response.

There was something so powerful that when Jesus walked by and said "Follow Me," Matthew left his tax collecting position. Peter, James, and John left their fishing business.

There is something so powerful about the mantle that is coming upon you that it will cause you to leave everything in order to follow the destiny God has for you.

3. It represented invested authority: The authority of God was invested in this mantle. Elijah had used it to smite rivers and cross on dry ground. He used it to perform the miraculous, for the mantle was symbolic of the authority of Almighty God which rested upon him.

THE MANTLE UPON JESUS

There is a mantle of divine intimacy, supernatural calling, and invested authority that God would place over His people today. That divine mantle is the mantle of the Holy Spirit.

When Jesus came to minister on this earth, God sent Him to destroy the works of the devil:

> ...For this purpose the Son of God was manifested, that he might destroy the works of the devil.

1 John 3:8

Jesus could not fulfill God's purpose in the flesh or His own strength, and neither can you! Jesus had to receive the mantle of the Holy Spirit before He could heal the sick and raise the dead. One day, down by the Jordan River, the mantle of God descended upon Him:

> And it came to pass in those days, that Jesus came from Nazareth of Galilee, and was baptized of John in Jordan. And straightway coming up out of the water, he saw the heavens opened, and the Spirit like a dove descending upon him: And there came a voice from heaven, saying, Thou art my beloved Son, in whom I am well pleased.

Mark 1:9-11

The mantle of the Holy Spirit descended upon Jesus in the form of a dove, symbolic of His divine calling. The heavens opened and God commissioned His Son to take up the mantle of His invested authority and begin to accomplish the purpose for which He had been sent to earth. God spoke concerning His pleasure in His beloved Son, confirming their relationship of divine intimacy.

THE MANTLE UPON US

Like the Prophet Elijah, Jesus placed His mantle upon His people before He returned to Heaven.

1.   It is a mantle of divine intimacy: Jesus said, *"And I will pray the Father, and he shall give you another Comforter, that he may abide with you for ever..."* (John 14:16).

The Comforter that Jesus sent was the Holy Spirit who was to abide with us and lead us into intimate relationship with God. The Holy Spirit teaches us all things, brings all things to our remembrance, and makes intercession through us according to the will of God. He serves so many purposes that we cannot even summarize them here, except to say that He leads us into a depth of intimacy with God not previously experienced by mankind.

2.   It is a mantle of supernatural calling: Jesus also said, *"...as my Father hath sent me, even so send I you"* (John 20:21). The mantle of God's purpose was passed from Jesus to us. Jesus commissioned us as He was sent–to do the same miracles, work the same works, and accomplish the same purposes. He told us to pick up the mantle of His calling and use it as He had used it.

3.   It is a mantle of invested authority: Through the Holy Spirit, Jesus also left us with the mantle of His invested authority:

> *And, behold, I send the promise of my Father upon you: but tarry ye in the city of Jerusalem, until ye be endued with power from on high.*

> Luke 24:49

Jesus told His disciples to wait in Jerusalem until they were endued with power. If they couldn't go out to minister to a lost and dying world without it, then neither can we!

It was this mantle of the Holy Spirit that empowered the early Church to accomplish its mission. Jesus said:

> *But ye shall receive power, after that the Holy Ghost is come upon you: and ye shall be witnesses unto me both in Jerusalem, and in all Judaea, and in Samaria, and unto the uttermost part of the earth.*

> Acts 1:8

Through the mantle of the Holy Spirit, we have the same authority Jesus had to do the works of God:

Then he called his twelve disciples together, and gave them power and authority over all devils, and to cure diseases. And he sent them to preach the kingdom of God, and to heal the sick.

Luke 9:1-2

Jesus has given us the mantle of invested authority over all the power of the enemy:

Behold, I give unto you power to tread on serpents and scorpions, and over all the power of the enemy: and nothing shall by any means hurt you.

Luke 10:19

God is calling forth a new generation, a new breed of people, and we are going to see even greater manifestations of the power and glory of God than Israel experienced. It will be greater than that of Elijah, for it is the double-portion anointing.

We have come to God, we have received, we have been blessed. Now it is time for us to take this mantle and pass it on to a multitude of Elishas who will minister to a lost and dying world.

CHAPTER THIRTEEN

PASSING ON THE MANTLE

*A*nd *it came to pass, when the Lord would take up Elijah into heaven by a whirlwind, that Elijah went with Elisha from Gilgal. And Elijah said unto Elisha, Tarry here, I pray thee; for the Lord hath sent me to Bethel. And Elisha said unto him, As the Lord liveth, and as thy soul liveth, I will not leave thee. So they went down to Bethel. And the sons of the prophets that were at Bethel came forth to Elisha, and said unto him, Knowest thou that the Lord will take away thy master from thy head to day? And he said, Yea, I know it; hold ye your peace. And Elijah said unto him, Elisha, tarry here, I pray thee; for the Lord hath sent me to Jericho. And he said, As the Lord liveth, and as thy soul liveth, I will not leave thee. So they came to Jericho. And the sons of the prophets that were at Jericho came to Elisha, and said unto him, Knowest thou that the Lord will take away thy master from thy head to day? And he answered, Yea, I know it; hold ye your peace. And Elijah said unto him, Tarry, I pray thee, here; for the Lord hath sent me to Jordan. And he said, As the Lord liveth, and as thy soul liveth, I will not leave thee. And they two went on. And fifty men of the sons of the prophets went, and stood to view afar off: and they two stood by Jordan. And Elijah took his mantle, and wrapped it together, and smote the waters, and they were divided hither and thither, so that they two went over on dry ground. And it came to pass, when they were gone over, that Elijah said unto Elisha, Ask what I shall do for thee, before I be taken away from thee. And Elisha said, I pray thee, let a double portion of thy spirit be upon me. And he said, Thou hast asked a hard thing: nevertheless, if thou see me when I am taken from thee, it shall be so unto thee; but if not, it shall not be so. And it came to pass, as they still went on, and talked, that, behold, there appeared a chariot of fire, and horses of fire, and parted them both asunder; and Elijah went up by a whirlwind into heaven. And Elisha saw it, and he cried, My father, my father, the chariot of Israel, and the horsemen thereof. And he saw him no more: and he took hold of his own clothes, and rent them in two pieces.*

1 Kings 2:1-12

Elijah's ministry does not end with the call of Elisha recorded in 1 Kings 19. For several years, he mentored Elisha, preparing him to receive the mantle of the anointing that would be passed on to him. Like Ruth and Naomi, David and Jonathan, their lives were joined together in one spirit and purpose.

There were several schools of the prophets, and Elijah began visiting and teaching in them, accompanied by Elisha who ministered to Elijah in humble service, ever at his side, ever learning. In order to lead, Elishas must learn how to be led. In order to serve, they must first become a servant.

Many political changes occurred during these years that Elijah and Elisha walked together. In 1 Kings 20:1-34 is the account of Israel's war with Syria, which lasted around two years, followed by three years of peace between Israel and Syria (1 Kings 22:1). During these years, Ahab joined forces with Syria to fight against Assyria, only to engage later in battle with Syria again. In 2 Kings 21 is a sad story of Ahab and Jezebel killing Naboth in order to seize his vineyard. Elijah's strong rebuke concerning this is found in 1 Kings 21:17-23.

Ahab died in a battle as predicted (1 Kings 22:1-38), and Jezebel also died as prophesied by Elijah. Their evil son ascended to the throne, following the pattern of his evil father and mother (1 Kings 22:52-53), and according to the word of the Lord spoken by Elijah, died soon after taking the throne of Israel (2 Kings 1:1-18).

During these tumultuous times, Elijah continued to be a strong prophetic voice, rebuking evil and declaring God's judgment. (For examples, see 2 Kings 1:15-16 and 21:17-23). The Elijah anointing is not just one that declares the reality of a compassionate God who saves souls, heals the sick, and raises the dead. The Elijah anointing also involves speaking out against the evil of leaders and nations and declaring in the name of God Almighty, "That is enough!"

God is looking for men and women who, like Elijah, will do things in the unconventional way–God's way. They will not care about reputation or position. They will be men and women who can deliver God's message in the spirit and power of Elijah, the power and anointing of the Holy Spirit.

Finally, there came the day when Elijah knew he was to be taken to Heaven and it was time for passing the mantle on to Elisha (2 King 2). Let us retrace their footsteps as Elijah literally walked Elisha into the mantle of the anointing, for there are many vital truths concealed in this account. There is prophetic purpose and meaning in each location they visited, and we must follow in their footsteps spiritually-speaking if we are to receive the mantle of this anointing.

GILGAL

And it came to pass, when the Lord would take up Elijah into heaven by a whirlwind, that Elijah went with Elisha from Gilgal. And Elijah said unto Elisha, Tarry here, I pray thee; for the Lord hath sent me to Bethel. And Elisha said unto him, As the Lord liveth, and as thy soul liveth, I will not leave thee.

2 Kings 2:1-2

Elijah and Elisha journeyed first to a place called Gilgal which represents foundational truths. This was the site between Jordan and Jericho where Israel first encamped after crossing the Jordan river and it was here that Joshua laid the foundation of the 12 stones of remembrance. It is the place of beginnings historically for Israel (Joshua 4:19-24).

To receive this anointing, you must first have the proper spiritual foundation. If you build your ministry on the shifting sands of man's opinion and methods, it will not stand. If you build upon the Rock, Christ Jesus, it will endure.

You must have a firm grasp of the basics: salvation, faith, baptism, laying on of hands, eternal judgment, resurrection, and miracles. But you cannot remain only at this foundational level. The Apostle Paul declared:

Therefore leaving the principles of the doctrine of Christ, let us go on unto perfection; not laying again the foundation of repentance from dead works, faith toward God, the doctrine of baptisms, laying on of hands, resurrection of the dead, and eternal judgment.

Hebrews 6:1-3

You cannot remain a milk-bottle believer, up and down, struggling with the basic truths of the Gospel. You must move on to the meat of the Word which represents spiritual maturity. Paul told the Hebrew believers:

For when for the time ye ought to be teachers, ye have need that one teach you again which be the first principles of the oracles of God; and are become such as have need of milk , and not of strong meat. For every one that useth milk is unskilful in the word of righteousness: for he is a babe. But strong meat belongeth to them that are of full age, even those who by reason of use have their senses exercised to discern both good and evil.

Hebrews 5:12-14

Get the basics right, so you can build the superstructure of your ministry on a firm foundation. The Apostle Paul declared:

According to the grace of God which is given unto me, as a wise masterbuilder, I have laid the foundation, and another buildeth thereon. But let every man take heed how he buildeth thereupon. For other foundation can no man lay than that is laid, which is Jesus Christ. Now if any man build upon this foundation gold, silver, precious stones, wood, hay, stubble; Every man's work shall be made manifest: for the day shall declare it, because it shall be revealed by fire; and the fire shall try every man's work of what sort it is. If any man's work abide which he hath built thereupon, he shall receive a reward. If any man's work shall be burned, he shall suffer loss: but he himself shall be saved; yet so as by fire.

1 Corinthians 3:10-15

Don't build on education, denomination, or tradition. Lay the foundation of your life and ministry on Jesus Christ, get the basics right, then build the superstructure. Many lives and ministries have collapsed during the storms of life because they didn't get the foundation right.

BETHEL

And the sons of the prophets that were at Bethel came forth to Elisha, and said unto him, Knowest thou that the Lord will take away thy master from thy head to day? And he said, Yea, I know it; hold ye your peace. And Elijah said unto him, Elisha, tarry here, I pray thee; for the Lord hath sent me to Jericho. And he said, As the Lord liveth, and as thy soul liveth, I will not leave thee...

2 Kings 2:3-4

The next place Elijah and Elisha visited is Bethel.

Bethel is a place of revelation: Bethel is first mentioned in Genesis 12:8 It is here that God appeared to Abraham with the revelation that his seed would inherit the promised land.

God will bring you to the place of revelation repeatedly, each time He wants to do a new thing in your life. But you cannot remain here. You must go forth and act upon the revelation you receive. If you tarry at the place of revelation, you will never see its manifestation.

Bethel is a place of worship: When Abraham visited Bethel, he built an altar and called upon the name of the Lord. You must learn to worship if you are to journey on with the prophet into this anointing.

Bethel is a place of renewal: After Abraham's tragic failure in Egypt, where he fell into lying and deceit, he knew where to go to make things right again. He returned to Bethel to renew his consecration to God (Genesis 13:3-4).

Bethel is a place of separation: God told Abraham to leave his family behind when he departed for the promised land, but Abraham took Lot along with him. God saw the weakness in Lot and knew it meant trouble for Abraham. The conflict between them eventually resulted in a parting of the ways. It was only after Lot departed that God once again spoke to Abraham, promising to make his seed as the dust of the earth. Who and what you hang on to and refuse to release can stifle God's revelation in your life.

Bethel is a place of decision: It was from Bethel that Lot viewed the cities of the Jordan. He saw, chose for himself, separated from the man of God, moved towards the world, and ended up sitting in the gates with ungodly elders and giving his daughters in marriage in Sodom. When Jacob first visited this same site, he had a powerful revelation, but he didn't really grasp it. He tried to bargain with God and wanted to build a memorial. On his second visit to Bethel, Jacob's life was changed when he finally surrendered to God. Bethel is a place of decision. It is not a place to build monuments and try to bargain with God.

JERICHO

...So they came to Jericho. And the sons of the prophets that were at Jericho came to Elisha, and said unto him, Knowest thou that the Lord will take away thy master from thy head today? And he answered, Yea, I know it; hold ye your peace. And Elijah said unto him, Tarry, I pray thee, here; for the Lord hath sent me to Jordan. And he said, As the Lord liveth, and as thy soul liveth, I will not leave thee. And they two went on.

2 Kings 2:4-6

Gilgal. Bethel. Still, Elijah and Elisha traveled on. Their next stop was Jericho, an important city which guarded the fords of the Jordan River. Jericho represents the appeal of the world and the flesh. You will recall that it was these cities which attracted Lot as he viewed them from Bethel.

Can you pass through Jericho with all its attractions of power, wealth, and position and go on to ford the Jordan to receive the power of God? Many men and women of God have established their foundations (Gilgal) and received a revelation from God (Bethel), only to succumb to the temptations of Jericho.

Jericho also represents the place of battle. It was here that Israel launched their invasion of the promised land (Joshua 4) and this was where Elijah battled with Ahab, Jezebel, and the evil prophets. This is not an easy anointing you are seeking. There will be tremendous spiritual battles. Do you really think that Satan is going to let you walk in this powerful anointing and receive the mantle of the double-portion without a fight?

JORDAN

And fifty men of the sons of the prophets went, and stood to view afar off: and they two stood by Jordan. And Elijah took his mantle, and wrapped it together, and smote the waters, and they were divided hither and thither, so that they two went over on dry ground.

2 Kings 2:7-8

Jordan is symbolic of death. Joshua and the people of Israel had to cross Jordan and die to the old life of Egypt and the wilderness wanderings. Elijah, too, must cross and Elisha must go through these waters. Even Jesus waded into the Jordan River; symbolic of death to the old life through water baptism.

Jordan was a barrier to their destination and it is symbolic of the barriers that would keep you from entering into the double-portion anointing. What is standing in your way? What is the "Jordan" that is hindering you from taking up this mantle? You must press through it if you are to receive the double-portion anointing.

You will note that in 2 Kings 2:7 there were 50 prophets who followed Elijah and Elisha from Jericho to Jordan, but only one received the mantle. That was the one who persevered on to cross over Jordan.

IT IS A HARD THING

This mantle we are learning about is a hard thing. The path to this anointing is not always convenient, and often is not logical. There was an easier, more direct route to their destination. But Elijah took the circuitous, more difficult route. Some commentators say there were schools of the prophets in these locations, and that he was making a final visit. That may be true, but we have also seen that he was walking out the prophetic purpose of the calling that Elijah was to receive.

Elisha might have been thinking:

- "This doesn't make sense."
- "We are backtracking."
- "Does Elijah really know where he is going?"
- "I could arrive at my destination quicker by doing it my own way."

God's way often goes through difficult paths and deep waters. His leading doesn't always make sense, but if you would receive the anointing, you must follow in the footsteps of the Master.

- As Joshua did with Moses.
- As Elisha with Elijah.
- As we must do with our Master, Jesus.

If you would receive the double-portion anointing, you must experience each of the places Elijah and Elisha visited symbolically in the spirit world. You must journey to Gilgal and get your foundations right. But you can't tarry there. You can't remain a baby Christian.

You must journey on to Bethel. You must make a decision to be separated to God, learn to worship Him, and receive new revelations. But you cannot remain there. Nor can you tarry at Jericho, with its promise of wealth, power, and fame. You must pass on through to Jordan. The place of death. You must learn to die daily to your own desires (1 Corinthians 15:31).

Like Jesus, you must die to the flesh in order to be quickened by the Spirit:

For Christ also hath once suffered for sins, the just for the unjust, that he might bring us to God, being put to death in the flesh, but quickened by the Spirit.

1 Peter 3:18

Elijah was involved in ministry right up to the moment the Lord took him. He continued to mentor Elisha as they walked along together. Those with the double-portion anointing do not retire. They simply leave this world in a blaze of glory, still ministering, still believing for the miraculous, still fulfilling dreams and revelations. And they leave behind them the mighty legacy of their mantle.

Did you notice that at each location–Gilgal, Bethel, Jericho, and Jordan–Elijah actually tried to discourage Elisha from continuing on with him? Elijah knew that the anointing Elisha sought was a difficult one. If you cannot pass the tests of Gilgal, Bethel, Jericho, and Jordan, then you will never receive the double-portion anointing.

But Elisha persevered and he and Elijah crossed Jordan together:

> And it came to pass, when they were gone over, that Elijah said unto Elisha, Ask what I shall do for thee, before I be taken away from thee. And Elisha said, I pray thee, let a double portion of thy spirit be upon me.

> 2 Kings 2:9

Elijah asked, "Before I leave, what is it you want?" Elisha did not ask for wealth, position, honor, or exemption from trouble. He simply asked to be qualified for service to God in order to reach his generation. He wanted a double-portion of the Spirit that rested upon his mentor. Is this your desire? The desires of your heart demonstrate how ready you are for the responsibility of this mantle.

"This is a hard thing you have asked," Elijah responded, "but if you remain with me, you will receive it." So the two friends continued on together, and suddenly:

> ...there appeared a chariot of fire, and horses of fire, and parted them both asunder; and Elijah went up by a whirlwind into heaven. And Elisha saw it, and he cried, My father, my father, the chariot of Israel, and the horsemen thereof. And he saw him no more: and he took hold of his own clothes, and rent them in two pieces.

> 2 Kings 2:11-12

As Elijah departed, Elisha witnessed it, but he was seeing more than his mentor being taken. He was seeing into the spirit world. As Elijah's mantle fluttered down, Elisha picked it up. He knew this sacred piece of cloth was a token of his divine mandate. He knew it was symbolic of his authority to carry on the work Elijah had begun.

Elijah was taken, but his mantle was not. His mantle remained.

If Jesus tarries, you and I may pass on, but we can leave behind the mantle of our anointing in the lives of men and women whom we have raised up for God.

Elijah tore his clothes and cried out in grief. But then he picked up the mantle and held it in his hands. What will he do? His mentor is gone and his heart is broken. Will he go back to farming? Will he question God's timing in removing the prophet? And how will he get back across the Jordan River?

Like Elisha, what is hindering you from entering into the double-portion anointing? Fear? Excuses? Unanswered questions? Grief? Barriers?

What will Elisha do? And even more importantly, what will YOU do?

CHAPTER FOURTEEN

WHERE IS THE LORD GOD OF ELIJAH?

Elisha took up also the mantle of Elijah that fell from him, and went back, and stood by the bank of Jordan; And he took the mantle of Elijah that fell from him, and smote the waters, and said, Where is the Lord God of Elijah? and when he also had smitten the waters, they parted hither and thither: and Elisha went over. And when the sons of the prophets which were to view at Jericho saw him, they said, The spirit of Elijah doth rest on Elisha. And they came to meet him, and bowed themselves to the ground before him. And they said unto him, Behold now, there be with thy servants fifty strong men; let them go, we pray thee, and seek thy master: lest peradventure the Spirit of the Lord hath taken him up, and cast him upon some mountain, or into some valley. And he said, Ye shall not send. And when they urged him till he was ashamed, he said, Send. They sent therefore fifty men; and they sought three days, but found him not. And when they came again to him, (for he tarried at Jericho,) he said unto them, Did I not say unto you, Go not?

2 Kings 2:13-18

We are never ready to lose our Elijah, but in order to enter into the next level of God's plan, at some point we must move beyond being mentored to putting into practice what we have learned:

- In the year that King Uzziah died, Isaiah received a new revelation of God.
- When Moses died, Joshua entered into the fulness of his ministry.
- When Saul was rejected, Samuel was directed by God to stop grieving, anoint a new king, and move on to the next part of God's plan.

This does not mean that a person must die, but there must come a time when Elisha takes up the mentor's mantle and begins to minister in the spirit and power of Elijah.

In the last chapter, we left Elisha standing gazing into the heavens after his departed mentor, holding Elijah's mantle which he had received as the chariot of fire took his master from him. This mantle was not just a keepsake or a treasured memory–it was a mantle of divine destiny and it was now in his hands. The question was, what would he do with it?

In the New Testament, the disciples were also left gazing into the heavens after their departed mentor, and they, too, received a divine mantle:

> *And Jesus came and spake unto them, saying, All power is given unto me in heaven and in earth. Go ye therefore, and teach all nations, baptizing them in the name of the Father, and of the Son, and of the Holy Ghost: Teaching them to observe all things whatsoever I have commanded you: and, lo, I am with you alway, even unto the end of the world. Amen.*

Matthew 28:18-20

The divine mandate of power Jesus left behind was the power of the Holy Spirit with which we are endued to carry on His work. It is the anointing of the Holy Spirit that takes you beyond the place of blessing into the realm of power. The mantle of this anointing is being passed into your hands. The question is, what will you do with it?

BEGIN TO ACT UPON THE ANOINTING

When you receive this mantle of the anointing, you must immediately act upon it as Elisha did. Elisha picked up the mantle and began where Elijah left off:

> *He (Elisha) took up also the mantle of Elijah that fell from him, and went back, and stood by the bank of Jordan; And he took the mantle of Elijah that fell from him, and smote the waters, and said, Where is the Lord God of Elijah? and when he also had smitten the waters, they parted hither and thither: and Elisha went over.*

2 Kings 2:13-14

Elisha took the mantle, representing the double-portion anointing, and walked to the banks of the river. Like Elijah, he took the mantle and smote the water, crying out "Where is the Lord God of Elijah." It was not Elijah he wanted, but the Lord God of Elijah. It was not the works of God he sought, but God Himself.

Psalm 103:7 indicates that the children of Israel knew God only by His acts, while Moses knew Him by His ways: *"He made known his ways unto*

Moses, his acts unto the children of Israel" (Psalm 103:7).

When Elijah struck the waters with the mantle, they immediately parted as they had for his mentor.

> *And when the sons of the prophets which were to view at Jericho saw him, they said, The spirit of Elijah doth rest on Elisha. And they came to meet him, and bowed themselves to the ground before him.*

2 Kings 2:15

There were 50 prophets of God watching from a distance on the other side of Jordan. When they saw the waters part for Elisha as they had for his mentor, they acknowledged that the spirit of Elijah rested upon him. When you receive the Elijah anointing, you won't have to advertise yourself as a prophet, evangelist, or teacher. People will recognize the manifestation of God's power in your life.

THE SPIRIT AND POWER OF ELIJAH

These same men, despite Elisha's protests, decided they would search for Elijah in the mountains, that surely he could not be gone:

> *And they said unto him, Behold now, there be with thy servants fifty strong men; let them go, we pray thee, and seek thy master: lest peradventure the Spirit of the Lord hath taken him up, and cast him upon some mountain, or into some valley. And he said, Ye shall not send. And when they urged him till he was ashamed, he said, Send. They sent therefore fifty men; and they sought three days, but found him not. And when they came again to him, (for he tarried at Jericho,) he said unto them, Did I not say unto you, Go not?*

2 Kings 2:16-18

Those standing at a distance never got it. They didn't realize what was happening between Elisha and Elijah. They did not receive the double-portion anointing, and they didn't even understand the finality of Elijah's departure. They went searching for the anointed one instead of receiving the anointing that one had left behind. They sought the prophet with the "big name." After all, Elijah was known for his miracles and his fantastic demonstration of power over the servants of Baal. They returned discouraged and sad because the mantle is not in Elijah–the mantle is *the spirit and power* of Elijah.

Do you want to be among those that stand afar, who are merely spectators of the things of God or do you want to be like Elisha, among those who receive the mantle of the double-portion anointing? If you want to receive the mantle of God's power, then you must be willing to follow Him all the way. You must cross over the "Jordans" of your life and conquer every barrier that is hindering your progress. You must begin to exercise with power and authority the divine anointing that has been placed in your hands.

CHAPTER FIFTEEN

HEALING THE WATERS

A nd the men of the city said unto Elisha, Behold, I pray thee, the situation of this city is pleasant, as my Lord seeth: but the water is naught, and the ground barren. And he said, Bring me a new cruse, and put salt therein. And they brought it to him. And he went forth unto the spring of the waters, and cast the salt in there, and said, Thus saith the Lord, I have healed these waters; there shall not be from thence any more death or barren land. So the waters were healed unto this day, according to the saying of Elisha which he spake.

2 Kings 2:19-22

One of the first miracles performed by Elisha was the healing of the waters. The men of a certain city came to Elisha and told him that the ground was barren because the water was no good. Elisha told them to bring him a new cruse with salt in it. Then he cast the salt into the spring, and declared, *"Thus saith the Lord, I have healed these waters; there shall not be from thence any more death or barren land"* (2 Kings 2:21), and the waters were healed as he commanded.

There is a great spiritual truth in this account of healing of the waters. Water in Scripture is a symbol of the Word that cleanses, refreshes, and gives life. Bad water portrays the opposite. The polluted waters in this story represent hurting humanity, men and women polluted by sin–those whose lives have been marred by adultery, fornication, murder, abuse, and every kind of evil. It is for this purpose that the mantle of the anointing rests upon us: To heal the waters of hurting humanity.

As in the natural example of Elisha healing the waters, it will take a new cruse. You cannot pour this anointing into the old vessels of tradition. Jesus declared:

And no man putteth new wine into old bottles: else the new wine doth burst the bottles, and the wine is spilled, and the bottles will be marred: but new wine must be put into new bottles.

Mark 2:22

Cleansing the waters will require salt. Salt in the Bible is used as a preservative that retards spoil, a seasoning, and a healing agent. As an Elijah who is taking a stand for God in this polluted world, you will be salt. Jesus declared:

> *Ye are the salt of the earth: but if the salt have lost his savour, wherewith shall it be salted? it is thenceforth good for nothing, but to be cast out, and to be trodden under foot of men.*

> Matthew 5:13

As salt in the world, you will retard evil. You will season the world with the Gospel and become God's healing agent. Salt also causes thirst. As you act as salt in the earth, men and women will thirst for the reality of the Gospel.

But remember: Salt, when it is put into a wound, causes pain. As you reach out to touch a polluted world, you may get negative reactions. Some people don't want to hear the truth because it hurts too much, but if you continue to do what Jesus said the salt will inevitably take affect.

To heal the waters required action. Elisha could have joined the men of the city in bemoaning their fate, but instead, he did something about it. It is time for God's people to rise up and take a stand against the pollution of this day. It is time for us to reach out and snatch people from the barren lands of sin and say to them, "Be healed!"

Notice that the cure of these waters was lasting, "*...unto this day...*" (2 Kings 2:22). The Bible declares that what God does, shall be forever (Ecclesiastes 3:14).

There was no more pollution, no more barren land. The Bible declares: "*Therefore if any man be in Christ, he is a new creature: old things are passed away; behold, all things are become new*" (2 Corinthians 5:17).

This is the message we must bear to the nations–your spiritually polluted land can be healed! This is the message to take to hurting humanity–the barren ground of your life can again be fruitful! The mantle is not placed in your hands as a sacred memento. It is not just a symbol. It represents the spirit and power of Elijah and Elisha. It will change lives. It can affect entire cities and nations.

A STREAM FROM GOD'S THRONE

In the book of Ezekiel 47:1-12, there is a record of another prophet at the banks of a stream:

> *Afterward he brought me again unto the door of the house; and, behold, waters issued out from under the threshold of the house eastward: for the forefront of the house stood toward the east, and the waters came down from under from the right side of the house, at the south side of the altar. Then brought he me out of the way of the gate northward, and led me about the way without unto the utter gate by the way that looketh eastward; and, behold, there ran out waters on the right side. And when the man that had the line in his hand went forth eastward, he measured a thousand cubits, and he brought me through the waters; the waters were to the ankles. Again he measured a thousand, and brought me through the waters; the waters were to the knees. Again he measured a thousand, and brought me through; the waters were to the loins. Afterward he measured a thousand; and it was a river that I could not pass over: for the waters were risen, waters to swim in, a river that could not be passed over. And he said unto me, Son of man, hast thou seen this? Then he brought me, and caused me to return to the brink of the river. Now when I had returned, behold, at the bank of the river were very many trees on the one side and on the other. Then said he unto me, These waters issue out toward the east country, and go down into the desert, and go into the sea: which being brought forth into the sea, the waters shall be healed. And it shall come to pass, that every thing that liveth, which moveth, whithersoever the rivers shall come, shall live: and there shall be a very great multitude of fish, because these waters shall come thither: for they shall be healed; and every thing shall live whither the river cometh. And it shall come to pass, that the fishers shall stand upon it from En-gedi even unto En-eglaim; they shall be a place to spread forth nets; their fish shall be according to their kinds, as the fish of the great sea, exceeding many. But the miry places thereof and the marishes thereof shall not be healed; they shall be given to salt. And by the river upon the bank thereof, on this side and on that side, shall grow all trees for meat, whose leaf shall not fade, neither shall the fruit thereof be consumed: it shall bring forth new fruit according to his months, because their waters they issued out of the sanctuary: and the fruit thereof shall be for meat, and the leaf thereof for medicine.*

Ezekiel 47:1-12

As we walk with the Prophet Ezekiel and his guide as they follow this stream, we note the following:

The waters came from the side of the altar: From the side of Jesus Christ flowed the blood and water as His life was sacrificed on the altar of Calvary. All that flows through us emanates from the altar. *"The streams proceed from the throne of God and the Lamb"* (Revelation 22:).

The waters were ever increasing: Some of us are content with a sprinkling of the power of God. Here we see that the living waters are ever increasing.

The waters increased by degrees: When they first tested the waters, it was to the ankles. Then to the knees. Then to the loins and, finally, deep enough to swim in–a river so deep it could not be passed over. The various depths of the waters also reflect the basics of the Christian walk:

- Ankles represent the walk of the believer in the Spirit.
- The knees represent the prayer life of the believer.
- The loins speak of girding up your loins for service and spiritual battle
- Waters to swim in represent the fulness of the Spirit.

On the brink of the river of God's anointing, will you be content with just ankle or knee deep waters–or will you jump into all God has for you and experience the fulness?

The waters from the sanctuary are running waters: They are not standing, stagnant waters. They are the living waters spoken of in John 4. They are fresh and new.

The waters signify the flow of God: The key to success in the Elijah anointing is to observe the direction God is moving and go with it.

The waters brought life: They ran to the Dead Sea, which was named that because nothing lived in it because there was no fresh water. Now, these rivers from the throne of God and His temple, bring life wherever they flow. When they enter the Dead Sea, the waters become fresh. The sea in scriptures symbolically refers to the nations. As the power of the Gospel flows through us, it brings life wherever it goes. Note that the Dead Sea, which before was shunned as noxious and barren, shall be frequented by fishermen. The Gospel makes those who were unprofitable become useful to both God and man.

There was a great multitude of fish: Because of the living waters, there was a great multitude of fish. Fishermen lined the banks to pull in the catch. In the Bible, fish are symbolic of men. Jesus called His disciples to be "fishers of men." When you immerse yourself in the depths of God, living water flows through you and a harvest of souls results.

There were trees of meat and miracles: Note the trees on the sides of the banks: This part of the vision is duplicated in St. John's vision in Revelation 22:2. Christians are called by Isaiah "trees of righteousness, the planting of the Lord." We are also instructed to be rooted in Him (Colossians 2:7).

As trees of the Lord we should serve the same purposes as these symbolic trees. They were for meat, which speaks of God's Word and having something with which to nourish the spiritually hungry. The trees were also for miracles of healing.

From Christ we draw the living waters and it produces both meat and miracles. We give the hungry the meat of God's Word and we bind up the broken and bruised.

The reason for this fruitfulness is because these waters issued out of the sanctuary, not from man made reservoirs. It was continual supply of living waters issuing from the throne of God.

To experience the fullness of these waters, you must launch out into the deep. Those who stay near the banks will remain in the salty marshes. Like Lot's wife, they will turn into a spiritual pillar of salt—one who looks back on the "good old days" instead of moving on with the flow of God.

In order to bear the fruit that feeds and heals, you must leave the marshes behind. You must launch out into the fulness of God. Like the Prophet Elisha, you must be able to deal with the polluted waters of the world and bring healing, deliverance, and life.

CHAPTER SIXTEEN

DEALING WITH THE OPPOSITION

*A*nd he went up from thence unto Bethel: and as he was going up
by the way, there came forth little children out of the city, and
mocked him, and said unto him, Go up, thou bald head; go up, thou
bald head. And he turned back, and looked on them, and cursed
them in the name of the Lord. And there came forth two she bears
out of the wood, and tare forty and two children of them. And he
went from thence to mount Carmel, and from thence he returned
to Samaria.

2 Kings 2:23-25

If you minister in the spirit and power of Elijah, you will experience
great challenges.

In the event described in 1 Kings 2:23-25, Elisha confronts direct
opposition. Anytime you are dong the work of God and declaring the
Word of God, you can except it. It simply goes with the territory. This is
one of the key lessons in these few verses. The messengers of God are not
always well-received by those lost in the darkness of sin:

*And this is the condemnation, that light is come into the world, and
men loved darkness rather than light, because their deeds were evil.
For every one that doeth evil hateth the light, neither cometh to
the light, lest his deeds should be reproved. But he that doeth truth
cometh to the light, that his deeds may be made manifest, that they
are wrought in God.*

John 3:19-21

Satan, who holds people in bondage, does not want them saved and
delivered. For this reason, the messengers of the Word become his target.

Following his ministry in Jericho, Elisha began to move out into the
land to minister to its inhabitants who were living in idolatry and greatly in
need of the Word. Elisha was on the way to Bethel, which means *"house of
God"* or *"place of God,"* speaking of worship and fellowship with God. There
was also a school of the prophets in Bethel, but in spite of this, the city was

idolatrous and anything but a center of worship. Hosea, who ministered years after Elisha, called this city Bethaven, meaning *"house of wickedness"* (Hosea 4:15; 5:8; 10:5).

The city of Bethel needed the Word to bring them back to the Lord.

The words *"and as he was going ..."* calls our attention to the time of the attack. It occurred in the normal process of his travel to the city. As you go forth in the spirit and power of Elijah to bear the Word to a lost world, the attacks will increase.

The description of *"little children"* in the King James Version, actually misses the true meaning in this passage. These were not children, but young men. The word *"lads" is the Hebrew "naar"* and was used of servants, soldiers, of Isaac when he was 28 years old, and of Joseph when he was 39 years old. This was like a modern-day gang of thugs, perhaps students of the false prophets.

This gang came out of the city and mocked Elisha, saying "Go up, you baldhead." "Mocked" is the Hebrew *"galas"* and denotes scornful belittling. Disrespect is one of the issues you will face repeatedly as you minister in this double-portion anointing.

These young men under Satan's influence were attacking not only Elisha, the man of God, but they were also attacking his message, the Word of God. They told Elijah to go up and called him "you bald head". Now whether or not Elisha was actually bald is immaterial. The point is, they were ridiculing the prophet and his message. Baldness was regarded as disgrace, for it was a usual consequence of leprosy, so in those days it was accounted a sign of personal and mental degradation.

THE MESSAGE AND THE MESSENGER

These attacks are typical of the methods Satan uses to attack the work of God. He attacks the message, the messenger, or both. He seeks to discredit both you and your message. This is why the miracle-working power of God is so important. Miracles confirm both the message and the messenger.

Most important in this account is Elisha's reaction and God's response. Elisha did not turn and run. He did not argue with them. He did not complain about the attack, nor did he debate with the young men. This teaches us that when trouble comes, we should never resort to the methods of the world.

Elisha simply cursed these mockers (2 Kings 2:24). This may seem out of character for the man of God, but you must remember–this was an attack upon the message and the messenger. It was not a personal squabble, but involved Elisha's divine destiny and the veracity of God Almighty. The key here is in the meaning of the word *"curse."* It does not mean to swear with dirty words, but it means to ask for the removal of the blessed state which brings God's protection, provision, and blessing.

Elisha saw that these rebellious youths were unresponsive to correction, so he simply turned them over to God. Immediately, two female bears came out of the brush and attacked the young men. God does not view lightly attacks upon His anointed servants.

As Elijahs and Elishas, we must expect opposition. As we go forth to minister to a lost and dying world, attacks will undoubtedly come. The Apostle Paul stated, *"In fact, everyone who wants to live a godly life in Christ Jesus will be persecuted..."* (2 Timothy 3:12 NIV). Paul preached the Gospel in the face of an angry mob (Acts 22:1-2); when falsely accused before rulers, he shared his faith (Acts 26:1-32); and when incarcerated, he wrote from prison to encourage others and continued to share his faith (Acts 16:29-34).

We need more men and women like Paul and like Elisha, who will stand fast, refuse to retreat, face confrontation head on and leave the results to the Lord.

FACING THE OPPOSITION

From the time of my first overseas crusade in Athens, Greece, I learned what it was to face opposition to preaching the Gospel of Jesus Christ. When I arrived in that country, the oppressive power of the government had hindered our contact there from securing a building for the meetings. The people were discouraged and defeated.

In the natural, the first reaction of many people who face a situation like this would be to start up through the proper channels of the bureaucratic chain of command until they found someone to change things. But God has never operated that way. The Apostle Paul declared:

For we wrestle not against flesh and blood, but against principalities, against powers, against the rulers of the darkness of this world, against spiritual wickedness in high places.

Ephesians 6:12

While natural inclinations were to seek the remedies of this world, I stayed in my hotel room and interceded until God moved. The battle was won, not in the courtrooms of Greek judges, but in the court of Heaven. The prime minister of Greece himself came to our assistance, secured a building, and we conducted a powerful crusade.

I learned that what seems to be an immovable object is always proven to be moveable when it meets the truly irresistible force of the hand of the living God. It was a lesson that would stick with me the rest of my life. When our natural inclination is to rely on people we think can help us, God's admonition is to rely on Him:

> *Thus saith the Lord; Cursed be the man that trusteth in man, and maketh flesh his arm, and whose heart departeth from the Lord. For he shall be like the heath in the desert, and shall not see when good cometh; but shall inhabit the parched places in the wilderness, in a salt land and not inhabited. Blessed is the man that trusteth in the Lord, and whose hope the Lord is.*

Jeremiah 17:5-7

In the early sixties, God sent me to Rosario, Argentina, to help pioneer the country for a move of the miracle-working power of God. I conducted mass crusades, preached the Word, and prayed for the sick. The Church had never seen such a manifestation of God's power. Blind eyes were opened, deaf ears were unstopped, the crippled and lame walked, and tumors and growths disappeared. It wasn't long until I was arrested and placed on trial for practicing medicine without a license!

Over the years of my ministry, I have faced almost every circumstance imaginable. I have been taken at gunpoint and questioned by Nicaraguan soldiers; I have preached two or three hours in a great downpour of rain until the water was ankle deep; I have preached while tanks roared down the streets of Porto Alegre, Brazil; and on one occasion in Argentina the police barricaded the streets to hold back over forty thousand people who were trying to enter the stadium where we were scheduled to conduct a meeting.

YOU CAN BE ASSURED OF VICTORY

Regardless of the opposition, I have never wavered because I know the calling God has placed upon my life. You must be assured of the calling God has placed upon you–the double-portion anointing, the spirit and power of Elijah–so you will never waver.

Expect opposition. The Bible declares, *"Yea, and all that will live godly in Christ Jesus shall suffer persecution"* (2 Timothy 3:12). Learn to use opposition as opportunity.

Elisha had no one to help when confronted with the gang of thugs, but he relied upon God and witnessed supernatural deliverance. If we place our trust in God as the prophet did, then difficult situations will allow us to witness the miraculous, delivering power of the living God.

CHAPTER SEVENTEEN

PREPARING FOR THE MOVE OF GOD

*N*ow Jehoram the son of Ahab began to reign over Israel in Samaria the eighteenth year of Jehoshaphat king of Judah, and reigned twelve years. And he wrought evil in the sight of the Lord; but not like his father, and like his mother: for he put away the image of Baal that his father had made. Nevertheless he cleaved unto the sins of Jeroboam the son of Nebat, which made Israel to sin; he departed not therefrom. And Mesha king of Moab was a sheepmaster, and rendered unto the king of Israel an hundred thousand lambs, and an hundred thousand rams, with the wool. But it came to pass, when Ahab was dead, that the king of Moab rebelled against the king of Israel. And king Jehoram went out of Samaria the same time, and numbered all Israel. And he went and sent to Jehoshaphat the king of Judah, saying, The king of Moab hath rebelled against me: wilt thou go with me against Moab to battle? And he said, I will go up: I am as thou art, my people as thy people, and my horses as thy horses. And he said, Which way shall we go up? And he answered, The way through the wilderness of Edom. So the king of Israel went, and the king of Judah, and the king of Edom: and they fetched a compass of seven days' journey: and there was no water for the host, and for the cattle that followed them. And the king of Israel said, Alas! that the Lord hath called these three kings together, to deliver them into the hand of Moab! But Jehoshaphat said, Is there not here a prophet of the Lord, that we may inquire of the Lord by him? And one of the king of Israel's servants answered and said, Here is Elisha the son of Shaphat, which poured water on the hands of Elijah. And Jehoshaphat said, The word of the Lord is with him. So the king of Israel and Jehoshaphat and the king of Edom went down to him. And Elisha said unto the king of Israel, What have I to do with thee? get thee to the prophets of thy father, and to the prophets of thy mother. And the king of Israel said unto him, Nay: for the Lord hath called these three kings together, to deliver them into the hand of Moab. And Elisha said, As the Lord of hosts liveth, before whom I stand, surely, were it not that I regard the presence of Jehoshaphat the king of Judah, I would not look toward thee, nor see thee. But now bring me a minstrel. And it came to pass, when the minstrel played, that the hand of the Lord came upon him. And he said, Thus saith the Lord, Make this valley full of ditches. For thus saith the Lord, Ye shall not see wind, neither shall ye see rain; yet that valley shall be filled with water, that ye may *drink, both ye, and your cattle, and your beasts. And this is but a light thing in the sight of the Lord: he will deliver the Moabites also into your hand. And ye shall smite every fenced city, and every choice city, and shall fell every good tree, and stop all wells of water, and mar every good piece of land with stones. And it came to pass in the morning, when the meat offering was offered, that, behold, there came water by the way of Edom, and the country was filled with water. And when all the Moabites heard that the kings were come up to fight against them, they gathered all that were able to put on armour, and upward, and stood in the border. And they rose up early in the morning, and the sun shone upon the water, and the Moabites saw the water on the other side as red as blood: And they said, This is blood: the kings are surely slain, and they have smitten one another: now therefore, Moab, to the spoil. And when they came to the camp of Israel, the Israelites rose up and smote the Moabites, so that they fled before them: but they went forward smiting the Moabites, even in their country. And they beat down the cities, and on every good piece of land cast every man his stone, and filled it; and they stopped all the wells of water, and felled all the good trees: only in Kir-haraseth left they the stones thereof; howbeit the slingers went about it, and smote it. And when the king of Moab saw that the battle was too sore for him, he took with him seven hundred men that drew swords, to break through even unto the king of Edom: but they could not. Then he took his eldest son that should have reigned in his stead, and offered him for a burnt offering upon the wall. And there was great indignation against Israel: and they departed from him, and returned to their own land.*

2 Kings 3:1-27

Upon the death of King Ahab, the nation of Moab rebelled against Israel and Ahaziah, the King who succeeded Ahab, did not make any attempt to stop them (2 Kings 1:1). His indifference resulted in great financial loss to Israel in terms of taxes and tributes. Finally, Ahaziah died in a fall through a lattice in the upper chamber of his house and his brother, Jehoram, inherited the throne of Israel (2 Kings 1:2).

Jehoram made a halfhearted attempt at spiritual reform by removing his father's idols and made plans to recover his brother's losses. Immediately after receiving the scepter to rule Israel, he arranged an expedition against Moab and sought the cooperation of Jehoshaphat, the king of Judah. The Moabites were heathen, idolatrous people whom God had subjugated under David's reign because of their threat to the national sovereignty of Israel. Spiritually, the Moabites represent the enemies that oppose the believer and his walk with God.

Jehoshaphat agreed to go up with Jehoram against Moab, and Israel and Judah united together against a common enemy. Jehoshaphat advised that they should not march the closest way over Jordan, but that they should go through the wilderness of Edom so that they might take the king of Edom (their tributary) and his forces along with them.

Before this great confederate army ever encountered the enemy, they were in danger of perishing for lack of water (2 Kings 3:9). The king of Israel sadly lamented the present distress, and Jehoshaphat suggested that they ask counsel of God, challenging, "Is there not here a prophet of the Lord, like unto Moses?"

IS THERE NO PROPHET OF THE LORD?

One of the king's servants answered and said, *"...Here is Elisha the son of Shaphat, which poured water on the hands of Elijah."* Then Jehoshaphat said, *"The word of the Lord is with him."* So, Jehoram, Jehoshaphat, and the king of Edom went to find Elisha to ask for a word from the Lord.

As the Church today faces the tremendous challenges and crises that have come upon the nations, Jehoshaphat's question again arises, *"Is there no prophet of the Lord here?"* There is a desperate need for the true prophetic ministry and the prophets God has called to stand and declare, *"Thus saith the Lord."* The Church needs people like Elisha with prophetic vision who can accurately discern what God is doing; who can hear what He is saying; who understand the times; and who can foresee what is coming. We need God-ordained prophets to warn, prepare, and position God's people to be victorious as we face the challenges of the closing days of time. This is a vital part of the Elijah anointing.

The prophetic ministry properly functioning within the Church is crucial for this hour. Throughout His dealings with mankind, God has always revealed what He was going to do through His prophets.

God entered into an intimate relationship with his prophets whereby He supernaturally revealed His plans, oftentimes through prophetic visions and dreams, so the prophets could warn the people of coming judgment.

- When God was ready to destroy Sodom and Gomorrah, He said, *"...Shall I hide from Abraham that thing which I do"* (Genesis 18:17)?

- He warned Abraham concerning the fiery judgment that was

coming, and was willing to withhold his judgment if there had been even one righteous person living there.

- He revealed to Joseph the seven years of famine that were coming upon the earth and how to prepare for them.

- He revealed to Moses the 10 plagues He was going to send upon Egypt.

- He revealed to Amos the downfall of Syria, Philistia, Tyre, Edom, Ammon, Moab, Judah, and Israel.

- Through many prophets, God revealed the destruction of Jerusalem and the captivity and dispersion of the Jews throughout the world.

- From Genesis through Malachi, God revealed the coming of the Messiah and the Kingdom of God.

- Through Jesus and many of the prophets, God has revealed the end-time events which will occur before Christ's second coming, the judgment coming upon the earth, and the end of the world.

God intends the Church to function from a position of knowing. He does not want to keep His plans hidden from us. He wants us to be prepared and living on the cutting edge of revelation.

If ever there was a day when the Church needs to hear godly men and women speaking the Word of the Lord it is today. We need those, called and anointed by God, who will go forth in the spirit and power of Elijah and speak God's message for the hour without fear or favor of man.

LESSONS FROM ELISHA

We can learn several important principles from these king's encounter with Elisha. The first thing we note is that Elisha was abrupt in his answer to Jehoram's inquiry. He said:

"What have I to do with thee? How canst thou expect an answer of peace from me? Get thee to the prophets of thy father and mother, whom thou hast countenanced and maintained in thy prosperity, and let them help thee now in thy distress"

2 Kings 3:13

Elisha was not impressed, as Jehoshaphat was, by Jehoram's partial reformation of putting away the images of Baal. In true reformation, the images should have been totally destroyed. At that very moment, the prophets of Baal were in Jehoram's camp.

God is not impressed by half-hearted attempts at obedience, and those who minister in the spirit and power of Elijah must be willing to say so and boldly proclaim, "Thus saith the Lord!"

Elisha showed respect to the godly king of Judah, however, and finally agreed that for his sake, he would enquire of the Lord. Elisha's mind was somewhat disturbed at the sight of Jehoram, so he called for a musician to play on his harp and sing psalms to the Lord. Whenever circumstances disturb your peace and you feel anxious or confused, began to praise and worship God as Elisha did. Confusion and anxiety will cease, and you will be able to hear clearly from the Lord.

Through Elisha, God assured the kings that although there would be no wind or rain, they would be supplied with the needed water. You will remember that the Prophet Elijah had prayed for rain, and it came the natural way. Here, God would supply water, but not in the traditional way of wind and rain. When you really enter into the double-portion anointing, you will learn that you can never limit God. You cannot put Him "in a box" and expect Him to move like He did in previous situations.

To test their faith and obedience, Elisha instructed the confederate army to dig ditches and prepare to receive the water. Those who expect to receive from the Lord must prepare for it, even when everything in the natural appears to be contrary to God's promises. Just remember–the deeper you dig spiritually, the more water you will be able to receive! God also promised the kings that supplying water was "*...a light thing in the sight of the Lord; you shall not only be saved from perishing, but shall return in triumph*" (2 Kings 3:18).

As prophesied by Elisha, the ditches were supernaturally filled with water. The water not only relieved the thirst of the languishing troops, but when the enemy army of Moab viewed the water in this normally dry valley from a distance, it looked like blood because it had been affected by the red soil. There had been no rain, so they didn't think it could possibly be water. They concluded that the confederacy of kings had turned on one another and that all they needed to do was swoop in and divide the spoils of war. The army of Moab rushed carelessly into the camp to plunder it and the confederate army of Israel, Judah, and Edom attacked, chased them into their own country, and destroyed their cities.

When the king of Moab realized that the capital city was about to fall into the hands of the enemy, he took 700 key warriors to attempt to open a way of escape. When this failed, the king took his eldest son, who was in line to succeed him, and offered him as a burnt-offering upon the wall (2 Kings 3:27). He did this to obtain the favor of his god, Chemosh, and to hopefully terrify the attacking army and cause them to retreat. There was great indignation against Israel because they had driven the king to such a terrible act, and the army reluctantly retreated.

LIVING WATERS

Did you observe what was said concerning Elisha in this passage? He ministered to Elijah by *"pouring water upon his hands"* (2 Kings 3:11). And have you noticed that several of Elisha's first miracles involved water? Elisha was humble enough to minister to Elijah by pouring water on his hands. Later on, Elisha was elevated to the parting of the Jordan, the healing of polluted waters, and now the filling of empty ditches with supernatural provision of water.

Christ's first miracle also involved water. Turning water into wine at the wedding feast was a humble act to minister to the needs of others. Later, Jesus would boldly announce, *"...but whosoever drinketh of the water that I shall give him shall never thirst; but the water that I shall give him shall be in him a well of water springing up into everlasting life"* (John 4:14).

And on the cross, water mingled with blood would flow from His side for the cleansing of sin and healing of our world.

Let us never forget: Our most important mission in The Elijah Institute is to take the living waters of Jesus Christ to a polluted world where empty ditches await the supernatural filling of the water of life. Whether the ministry be humble to one individual or spectacular to the multitudes, the mission is the same. Living water must flow through us to meet the needs of others.

Prepare to receive it. Break open the ground of your hardened heart. Dig your spiritual ditches and prepare for the supernatural move of God.

CHAPTER EIGHTEEN

FILLING EMPTY VESSELS

Now there cried a certain woman of the wives of the sons of the prophets unto Elisha, saying, Thy servant my husband is dead; and thou knowest that thy servant did fear the Lord: and the creditor is come to take unto him my two sons to be bondmen. And Elisha said unto her, What shall I do for thee? tell me, what hast thou in the house? And she said, Thine handmaid hath not any thing in the house, save a pot of oil. Then he said, Go, borrow thee vessels abroad of all thy neighbours, even empty vessels; borrow not a few. And when thou art come in, thou shalt shut the door upon thee and upon thy sons, and shalt pour out into all those vessels, and thou shalt set aside that which is full. So she went from him, and shut the door upon her and upon her sons, who brought the vessels to her; and she poured out. And it came to pass, when the vessels were full, that she said unto her son, Bring me yet a vessel. And he said unto her, There is not a vessel more. And the oil stayed. Then she came and told the man of God. And he said, Go, sell the oil, and pay thy debt, and live thou and thy children of the rest.

2 Kings 4:1-7

She was a woman in desperate circumstances. She was a widow with no source of income to meet the needs of her family. She was in debt, and as was the custom of the times, the creditor had come to take her two sons as slaves as payment for the bill. In her time of desperate need, this woman knew only one thing. She knew she must get to the man of God, Elisha. As you begin to minister in the spirit and power of Elijah, people will come to you with desperate needs and you must be in a position to give them answers from God.

Elisha questioned the woman, "What do you have of value in your house?" She responded that all she had was a pot of oil. Elisha directed her to go and borrow vessels from her neighbors, enter into her house, shut the door, and begin to pour the oil into the vessels.

The widow acted upon the word of the Lord spoken through His prophet, Elisha. She gathered the vessels and brought them to her house. She shut the door to the outside world of famine and fear, and began to pour the oil. One vessel. Two vessels. Three vessels filled. As long as there were empty vessels, she continued to pour and the oil continued to multiply. She sold the oil, paid the debt, and her sons were freed from their obligation.

God generally meets our needs by taking what we have and multiplying it as we turn it to Him and obey His Word. Beyond the fact that God will provide our financial needs, however, there is a tremendous message in this account that is vital to those walking in the spirit and power of Elijah. As long as there were empty vessels, the oil continued to multiply. The flow only ceased when there were no more empty vessels.

As long as you are pouring your life into empty vessels–those who are in need, those bound by sin and addiction, the unloved, the rejected–the oil of God's anointing and provision will continue to flow through you. It will only be limited by the number of empty vessels. As long as you are investing your life into the empty vessels of hurting humanity, the double-portion anointing oil of the Holy Spirit will continue to flow.

YOUR SOURCE WILL NEVER BE EXHAUSTED

Don't look around at all the needs and question, "How can I ever fill all these vessels?" Let the anointing oil of the Holy Spirit flow through you and you will never run dry, your source will never be exhausted, and you will never burn out. It will be a continual supply of the anointing. The Prophet Zechariah explains this process:

And the angel that talked with me came again, and waked me, as a man that is wakened out of his sleep, And said unto me, What seest thou? And I said, I have looked, and behold a candlestick all of gold, with a bowl upon the top of it, and his seven lamps thereon, and seven pipes to the seven lamps, which are upon the top thereof: And two olive trees by it, one upon the right side of the bowl, and the other upon the left side thereof. So I answered and spake to the angel that talked with me, saying, What are these, my lord? Then the angel that talked with me answered and said unto me, Knowest thou not what what these be? And I said, No, my lord. Then he answered and spake unto me, saying, This is the word of the Lord unto Zerubbabel, saying, Not by might, nor by power, but by my spirit, saith the Lord of hosts. Who art thou, O great mountain? before Zerubbabel thou shalt become a plain: and he shall bring forth the headstone thereof with shoutings, crying, Grace, grace unto it. Moreover the word of the Lord came unto me, saying, The hands of Zerubbabel have laid

the foundation of this house; his hands shall also finish it; and thou shalt know that the Lord of hosts hath sent me unto you. For who hath despised the day of small things? for they shall rejoice, and shall see the plummet in the hand of Zerubbabel with those seven; they are the eyes of the Lord, which run to and fro through the whole earth. Then answered I, and said unto him, What are these two olive trees upon the right side of the candlestick and upon the left side thereof? And I answered again, and said unto him, What be these two olive branches which through the two golden pipes empty the golden oil out of themselves? And he answered me and said, Knowest thou not what these be? And I said, No, my lord. Then said he, These are the two anointed ones, that stand by the Lord of the whole earth.

Zechariah 4:1-14

The ministry of Zechariah was exercised among the remnant of the Jews after their return from 70 years in captivity in Babylon. God gave him several visions to meet the needs of the struggling colony. The visions were specifically adapted to the trials and circumstances of the time, but also have broader significance than their original purpose.

In the vision described in this passage, Zechariah saw a lamp stand (like a menorah) with a bowl on top of it filled with oil. Seven channels or pipes extended from this bowl to each of the seven lights making 490 channels in all–an abundant provision. There were no oil cans, no clumsy attendants filling the reservoirs. On each side, there was an olive tree supplying the oil.

There are two levels of interpretation of this prophetic vision. One concerns the nation of Israel. The lamp stand represented Israel who was to bear the light of God. The olive trees represent Joshua and Zerubbabel, the two instruments God would use to bring light back into Israel and make them a light to the world. The vision was also given to encourage Zerubbabel to finish building the temple.

WE BEAR THE LIGHT

Although the vision had an immediate fulfillment at that time, it also applies to us today. The church is the lamp stand and we are to be light bearers to the world. The two trees represent the Holy Spirit from the Father and Christ with the Father, the two sources of anointing. The oil is a type of the Holy Spirit who gives light, life, and energy. We learn several lessons from this in regards to the anointing of God:

God's power will accomplish God's purposes. Oil is one of the most clearly defined symbols in the Bible representing the Holy Spirit. The bowl acts as a reservoir for the constant, abundant flow. Silently, without the assistance of human force, the Spirit works without might or power: *"So he said to me, This is the word of the Lord to Zerubbabel: Not by might nor by power, but by My Spirit,' says the Lord Almighty"* (Zechariah 4:6 NIV).

"Might" and "power" as used here are general terms for resources such as physical strength, human ability, efficiency, or wealth. We cannot minister in our own wisdom, power, or might. The anointing of the Holy Spirit must flow through us.

Opposition will be conquered. The declaration is made, *"Who art thou, O great mountain? Before Zerubbabel thou shalt become a plain"* (Zechariah 4:7). The mountains represent opposition and God promises that all the difficulties they represent shall be removed.

God will finish in us and through us what He starts. The Word declares:

> *...And he shall bring forth the capstone with shouts of "Grace, grace to it!" Moreover the word of the Lord came to me, saying: "The hands of Zerubbabel have laid the foundation of this temple; his hands shall also finish it." Then you will know that the Lord of hosts has sent Me to you.*

> Zechariah 4:7-9

The headstone is the finishing stone which marks the completion of the project. The Apostle Paul declared that we could be *"...confident of this very thing, that He who has begun a good work in you will complete it until the day of Jesus Christ"* (Philippians 1:6, NKJ). It is the Spirit's energy in us that enables us to not become weary in well doing. It is the Spirit that enables us to say, "I have fought a good fight, I have finished the work, I was not disobedient to the heavenly vision."

God uses small things/feeble instruments. Americans often measure success by the size of the building, the crowds, etc. We must quit despising small things. Few of you know the name of Mrs. Kerr who led me to the saving knowledge of the Messiah, but what a great legacy of souls this woman has in the Kingdom of God because of what God has done through my life. In God's work, the day of small things is not to be despised:

*For who has despised the day of small things? For these seven rejoice
to see the plumb line in the hand of Zerubbabel. They are the eyes of
the Lord, which scan to and fro throughout the whole earth.*

Zechariah 4:10 NKJ

God often chooses weak and unlikely instruments to bring about great
things and He always measures our success by the plumb line of His Word,
not by worldly standards.

The lessons of this chapter are many. You must let oil continue to
flow through you to fill the empty vessels of human lives. Let God's power
accomplish His purposes. Know that God will conquer all opposition,
He will use even small and feeble instruments, and He will finish in and
through us what He starts.

CHAPTER NINETEEN

HOW TO RAISE THE DEAD

*A*nd it fell on a day, that Elisha passed to Shunem, where was a great woman; and she constrained him to eat bread. And so it was, that as oft as he passed by, he turned in thither to eat bread. And she said unto her husband, Behold now, I perceive that this is an holy man of God, which passeth by us continually. Let us make a little chamber, I pray thee, on the wall; and let us set for him there a bed, and a table, and a stool, and a candlestick: and it shall be, when he cometh to us, that he shall turn in thither. And it fell on a day, that he came thither, and he turned into the chamber, and lay there. And he said to Gehazi his servant, Call this Shunammite. And when he had called her, she stood before him. And he said unto him, Say now unto her, Behold, thou hast been careful for us with all this care; what is to be done for thee? wouldest thou be spoken for to the king, or to the captain of the host? And she answered, I dwell among mine own people. And he said, What then is to be done for her? And Gehazi answered, Verily she hath no child, and her husband is old. And he said, Call her. And when he had called her, she stood in the door. And he said, About this season, according to the time of life, thou shalt embrace a son. And she said, Nay, my Lord, thou man of God, do not lie unto thine handmaid. And the woman conceived, and bare a son at that season that Elisha had said unto her, according to the time of life. And when the child was grown, it fell on a day, that he went out to his father to the reapers. And he said unto his father, My head, my head. And he said to a lad, Carry him to his mother. And when he had taken him, and brought him to his mother, he sat on her knees till noon, and then died. And she went up, and laid him on the bed of the man of God, and shut the door upon him, and went out. And she called unto her husband, and said, Send me, I pray thee, one of the young men, and one of the asses, that I may run to the man of God, and come again. And he said, Wherefore wilt thou go to him to day? it is neither new moon, nor sabbath. And she said, It shall be well. Then she saddled an ass, and said to her servant, Drive, and go forward; slack not thy riding for me, except I bid thee. So she went and came unto the man of God to mount Carmel. And it came to pass, when the man of God saw her afar off, that he said to Gehazi his servant, Behold, yonder is that Shunammite: Run now, I pray thee, to meet her, and

*say unto her, Is it well with thee? is it well with thy husband? is it
well with the child? And she answered, It is well. And when she
came to the man of God to the hill, she caught him by the feet: but
Gehazi came near to thrust her away. And the man of God said, Let
her alone; for her soul is vexed within her: and the Lord hath hid it
from me, and hath not told me. Then she said, Did I desire a son of
my Lord? did I not say, Do not deceive me? Then he said to Gehazi,
Gird up thy loins, and take my staff in thine hand, and go thy way:
if thou meet any man, salute him not; and if any salute thee, answer
him not again: and lay my staff upon the face of the child. And the
mother of the child said, As the Lord liveth, and as thy soul liveth,
I will not leave thee. And he arose, and followed her. And Gehazi
passed on before them, and laid the staff upon the face of the child;
but there was neither voice, nor hearing. Wherefore he went again
to meet him, and told him, saying, The child is not awaked. And
when Elisha was come into the house, behold, the child was dead,
and laid upon his bed. He went in therefore, and shut the door
upon them twain, and prayed unto the Lord. And he went up, and
lay upon the child, and put his mouth upon his mouth, and his
eyes upon his eyes, and his hands upon his hands: and he stretched
himself upon the child; and the flesh of the child waxed warm. Then
he returned, and walked in the house to and fro; and went up, and
stretched himself upon him: and the child sneezed seven times, and
the child opened his eyes. And he called Gehazi, and said, Call this
Shunammite. So he called her. And when she was come in unto him,
he said, Take up thy son. Then she went in, and fell at his feet, and
bowed herself to the ground, and took up her son, and went out.*

2 Kings 4:8-37

One of the most outstanding miracles God performed in answer
to Elisha's prayers was the raising of the Shunammite's son from the
dead. Elisha was a frequent guest in the special room prepared by this
Shunammite woman. When Elisha learned that she did not have a son and
that her husband was quite elderly and beyond child-producing years, he
prophesied that she would conceive and bear a son (2 Kings 4:16).

As Elisha prophesied, the woman had a son, years passed, and the child
grew. One day, as the boy was out in the fields with his father, he became
sick and died. The Shunammite woman took him up to the room where
the prophet stayed when he was in town and laid him on the prophet's
bed. She quickly saddled a donkey and set out with her servant to go to
Elisha where he was staying at Mt. Carmel. Her son was dead. Imagine the
thoughts that flooded her mind. "Why had this happened? Why had God

allowed the son He had given her to die?"

Although her boy's lifeless body was upstairs lying on the bed, she did not keep her eyes on her desperate situation. She believed that if she could just get to Elisha, the prophet of God, he would be able to help her. She hurriedly prepared for her journey, and as she departed she told her husband, "...*It is well,*" in answer to his questions (2 Kings 4:23).

When Elisha saw the woman coming at a distance, he sent Gehazi, his servant, to meet her and ask if everything was all right. The Lord had not yet revealed to Elisha the purpose for her visit. The woman answered that all was well, but when she saw Elisha she ran to him and fell at his feet. Gehazi tried to push her away, but Elisha told him to leave her alone.

"Did I ask you for a son? Didn't I tell you, do not deceive me?" the woman cried out in anguish (2 Kings 4:28). Immediately, Elisha told Gehazi to take his staff in his hand and run to the Shunammite's house to minister to the boy. But the Shunammite woman refused to leave Elisha's side. She was desperate! She was determined to persevere until Elisha agreed to go with her. He was a prophet of God and she wanted him to cry out to God for the life of her boy (2 Kings 4:30). When Elisha saw her determination, he finally agreed to go.

THE POWER OF PERSEVERANCE

This Shunammite woman was determined to persevere in behalf of her son regardless of the seemingly impossible circumstances. What are the obstacles standing in the way of your pressing through in prayer to receive your miracle? What are the obstacles that are hindering you from ministering in the spirit and power of Elijah? Whatever need you face–whether it be a personal need, a financial need, or a physical challenge– get your eyes off your circumstances and onto the faithfulness of God. Your faith must not be limited by your need, your own limited abilities, or by what you see with your natural eyes.

Jesus taught that we are to believe we have received what we have asked when we pray. He said, "... *What things soever ye desire, when ye pray, believe that ye receive them, and ye shall have them*" (Mark 11:24). By eyes of faith, begin to see beyond the natural into the supernatural realm where all things are possible with God.

Gehazi went ahead of Elisha and the boy's mother, entered the room where the boy's lifeless body lay on the bed, and placed Elisha's staff on the boy's face. Nothing happened.

Gehazi went to meet Elisha and told him that the boy had not awakened (2 Kings 4:31). This did not stop Elisha or the mother. They didn't give up. Elisha knew God's power was stronger than death.

When Elisha reached the house, he went into his room and shut the door. Alone in the room, facing the boy's corpse, he began to cry out to God with great fervency. We do not know how long he prayed, but he prayed until he knew God had heard and answered.

After Elisha prayed, he spread himself over the boy's body. The life of God began to flow through him into the boy and his body grew warm, but he was still lifeless. Elisha got up and walked back and forth in the room. A second time Elisha stretched himself on the boy's lifeless body and suddenly the power of God broke the chains of death. The life of God entered the boy, raised him from the dead, and he sneezed seven times as the breath of life entered into him. Elisha sent for the Shunammite woman and presented her son to her alive and well.

RAISING THE SPIRITUALLY DEAD

In this account of Elisha raising this boy from the dead, there are spiritual truths that can be applied to spreading the Gospel. Evangelism is a natural parallel of raising the dead because you rescue people from the eternal destiny of spiritual death. The Bible says the soul that sins will die, that the wages of sin is death, and that sinners are dead in transgressions and sin. The following spiritual applications can be drawn from this account and may be applied as you go forth to raise the spiritually dead.

You must have faith. The mother did not just accept the child's death. The normal response would be to weep, call professional mourners, and prepare the body for burial. Instead, she laid him on Elisha's bed, shut the door, and went to get the prophet.   To understand this, you must recall the account in 1 Kings 17:17-24 where Elijah raised a young man from the dead. Taking the child to the prophet's chamber was an act of faith recalling the well-known miracle previously done by Elijah. She did not wait for the prophet to take him into the room. She took him in, expecting a miracle. God has raised spiritually dead men from the beginning of time. We must take unsaved people, just as they are, to the place of a miracle.

Note this woman's faith when she said in answer to her husband's questions, *"It shall be well"* (2 Kings 4:23-24). When you begin to act by faith, your faith increases. By the time she neared the prophet, her faith had increased (2 Kings 4:26). When Elisha sent his servant Gehazi to question her, she no longer said, *"It shall be well."* She said, *"It is well."*

You must make haste. Note in 2 Kings 4:22 that the woman said, *"That I may run."* You must make haste to raise the dead because souls are dying in sin–right now, today, this very hour.

You must break with tradition. In 2 Kings 4:23, the woman's husband questioned, "Why are you going?" It was not the traditional time to go to the prophet. It was not the new moon or Sabbath. You may have to break with tradition to evangelize in the demonstration of God's power. People may tell you, "This is not the way we do things."

You must have compassion. The dead will never be raised by "Gehazis" who have no compassion (2 Kings 4:25-27). When the woman came in search of life, he would have sent her away, but the Prophet of God showed concern. He asked, "Is it well with you and your husband and the child?"

There are people who have struggled "up the hill" to get to us. They are falling at our feet with great needs, yet we thrust them away. We send them to secular counselors, recommend medication, or suggest rehabilitation centers. We must have compassion on them and not turn them away. We must have enough of the spirit and power of Elijah that we can minister to their desperate needs.

You must go where they are. To help those dead in sin, you must go where they are, just as Elisha went to the young child.

We cannot send powerless men (like Gehazi) or substitute measures (represented by the staff). This mother would settle for no substitutes. Dying men and women can settle for nothing other than the power of God that is able to breathe new life into a dead soul. To raise us from the death of sin, Jesus came into this world. He came where we were. We too must go to the lost with the message of life.

If you are to raise the dead, you must follow the master's example to go where they are. In 1 Kings 17:17-24, the Bible records the story of Elijah, who had been Elisha's master, setting the example for raising a dead child. If Elisha had followed that example, he never would have sent Gehazi with his staff to try to do the job.

Elisha thought that God's power could work without his personal presence and efforts, so he sent his staff with Gehazi. We take doctrinal or practical truth and lay them upon the spiritually dead, but we do not personally become involved with them. We try many methods apart from personal involvement, but we will have no more effect upon a lost soul than did Elisha's staff.

The letter of the law without the Spirit will never raise dead men. Life will not flow as long as leadership is placing an indifferent hand upon dead men and women. We must get out of the pews and into the darkness of this world where the dead are–the prisons, drug houses, places of prostitution, etc.

You must recognize the seriousness of the condition. Gehazi did not really believe the child was dead. He reported back, "The child is not waked." Gehazi spoke as if the boy was only asleep, but Elisha knew the child was dead (2 Kings 4:32). Unbelievers lost in sin are not just sleeping. It is a serious condition. It is spiritual death, and they will never be raised until we recognize this fact.

You must not be defeated by failure. The first attempt to raise the dead child through Gehazi failed. When you fail in one attempt, do not give up. Do not infer from failure that you are not called to the task. The lesson of failure is not withdrawing from the mission, but persevering and changing your methods to follow the example of the Master.

You must resurrect life in the inner chamber. Elisha went into the inner chamber, the place where he regularly prayed to God. You must go into the "inner chamber" of prayer, shut the door, and intercede for dying humanity.

You must be endued with power. As he entered into that inner chamber, Elisha already knew the source of his power. The mantle of the anointing rested upon him, Elisha knew his source of power, and it was tried and proven.

You must know the objective. Your objective is not to cleanse a dead body, embalm it with spices, or cover it with fine linen. These are all improvements, but you still have a dead body. Your objective is not to teach self-improvement or change society. Your objective is new spiritual life!

You must be alive yourself. Dead men can't raise the dead. Elisha stooped over the corpse and placed his mouth upon the mouth of the dead child. He placed his eyes upon its eyes, his hands upon its hands. The warm body of the man of God covered the cold body of the child. If you are to raise the dead, you must come into contact with death. When Jesus would raise us from spiritual death, He came into this world of sin and death and died Himself. If you will raise the dead, you must feel the chill and horror of their condition–spiritual death.

As Elisha covered death with life, the warmth of his body entered the child. If you are dead yourself, this will not happen. Placing one corpse upon another is hopeless. It is vain for dying people to gather around another dead soul and expect resurrection.

You must be willing to be stretched. One would think a grown man would have to contract himself on a child, but instead it says he stretched himself. Reaching out to dying men and women is a stretching experience. You must leave your home and the security of your Christian friends and environment. You must step out of your comfort zone.

You must settle for nothing less than life. In 2 Kings 4:34, it indicates that the flesh of the child became warm, but Elisha did not just settle for this sign of life. He would settle for nothing less than true life. It is not lukewarmness we are after, but life! Not mere emotionalism, but true revival!

Elisha walked back and forth, waiting and no doubt calling upon God. Then he stretched himself upon the child again. This time, the child sneezed seven times. (The word *sneeze* actually means *gasped*). As the child gasped, new life entered his body and his eyes opened. When dead men and women gasp into their beings the saving power of the mighty rushing wind of the Holy Spirit, they too will experience new life.

Elisha took the child and returned him to the arms of his loving mother, alive and well. Our divine mission is to take dying men and women, breathe into them the breath of life of salvation, and return them to the arms of their Heavenly Father, alive and well.

CHAPTER TWENTY

THE GOD WHO PROVIDES

*A*nd Elisha came again to Gilgal: and there was a dearth in the land; and the sons of the prophets were sitting before him: and he said unto his servant, Set on the great pot, and seethe pottage for the sons of the prophets. And one went out into the field to gather herbs, and found a wild vine, and gathered thereof wild gourds his lap full, and came and shred them into the pot of pottage: for they knew them not. So they poured out for the men to eat. And it came to pass, as they were eating of the pottage, that they cried out, and said, O thou man of God, there is death in the pot. And they could not eat thereof. But he said, Then bring meal. And he cast it into the pot; and he said, Pour out for the people, that they may eat. And there was no harm in the pot. And there came a man from Baal-shalisha, and brought the man of God bread of the firstfruits, twenty loaves of barley, and full ears of corn in the husk thereof. And he said, Give unto the people, that they may eat. And his servitor said, What, should I set this before an hundred men? He said again, Give the people, that they may eat: for thus saith the Lord, They shall eat, and shall leave thereof. So he set it before them, and they did eat, and left thereof, according to the word of the Lord.*

2 Kings 4:38-44

Two great miracles are recorded in this passage, both occurred during a famine, and both are vital to the understanding of our mission to the world.

HEALING OF THE POISONOUS STEW

The sons of the prophets were gathered before Elisha, presumably to be mentored by him, and Elisha gave orders that a big pot of stew be prepared for them. One of the cooks went out in a field and picked some wild gourds to add to the stew, but they turned out to be poisonous. The world is filled with poisonous ideologies. To the spiritually blind, they look good, but they are actually full of death.

When the stew was served, the men immediately realized that it was poison. Elisha requested that meal be brought and cast into the pot, then he commanded, *"...Pour out for the people, that they may eat. And there was no harm in the pot"* (2 Kings 4:41).   In order to live, the men must now eat of the life-giving pot of stew.

The flour which Elisha cast into the poisonous stew is symbolic of the Lord Jesus and His Word which are the only antidotes to the poisons of this world. *"And Jesus said unto them, I am the bread of life: he that cometh to me shall never hunger"* (John 6:35).

> *Verily, verily, I say unto you, He that believeth on me hath everlasting life. I am that bread of life. Your fathers did eat manna in the wilderness, and are dead. This is the bread which cometh down from heaven, that a man may eat thereof, and not die. I am the living bread which came down from heaven: if any man eat of this bread, he shall live for ever: and the bread that I will give is my flesh, which I will give for the life of the world.*
>
> John 6:47-51

One must either feed on the Lord Jesus Christ or die from the poisonous pottage of the world.

When you go out to a lost and dying world, poisoned by the pollution of sin which leads to death, you cannot go with your own ideas. You cannot simply take a rehabilitation plan or a 12-step program. You must bear the living bread that will reverse the effects of the "death in the pot" of this world. You must share the bread that came down from Heaven, Jesus Christ, who gave His life to reverse the effects of sin and death. God has already provided a solution to the "death in the pot", and it is Jesus Christ. All who eat of the bread you share will live!

SUPERNATURAL MULTIPLICATION OF FOOD

The second miracle involved the multiplication of loaves of bread and ears of corn. An unnamed man from Baal-shalisha came to offer Elisha the first-fruits of his labors which was twenty loaves of barley and full ears of corn. It is interesting that *shalisha* means a third and can mean the "Lord who multiplies." This man brought what he had, and that is always enough when placed in the hands of God.

Elisha commanded the server to give this food to the people to eat. His response was, *"What, should I set this before an hundred men?"* This man had the wrong perspective. He was looking at the meager resources in his hands. He was looking to self... *"What should I set before them...."* The work God is calling you to is too great for your own meager resources. It is not your ministry. It is the work of God through you. Don't be afraid at God's command to spiritually invite a multitude to dinner. You have the bread of life and it will be sufficient.

Elisha commanded him again, *"...Give the people, that they may eat: for thus saith the Lord, They shall eat, and shall leave thereof"* (2 Kings 4:43). The server obeyed, set the food before the crowd, they ate until they were full, and still had leftovers (2 Kings 4:38-44).

This miracle reflects similar events in the ministry of Jesus where bread and fish were multiplied to feed the multitudes (Matthew 14 and 15). Despite these miracles, as Jesus and His disciples journeyed on, the disciples were fretting because they forgot to take along bread:

> *And they reasoned among themselves, saying, It is because we have taken no bread. Which when Jesus perceived, he said unto them, O ye of little faith, why reason ye among yourselves, because ye have brought no bread? Do ye not yet understand, neither remember the five loaves of the five thousand, and how many baskets ye took up? Neither the seven loaves of the four thousand, and how many baskets ye took up?*

Matthew 16:7-10

How soon they forgot the miraculous provision they had witnessed.

GOD WILL PROVIDE

Get this settled in your heart once and for all. The same God who healed the poisonous stew, the same God who multiplied bread and corn for the sons of the prophets, and the same God who increased the loaves and fishes–He is the one who will provide for you as you go forth to minister in the spirit and power of Elijah.

Do not look to man. Do not look to the meager provision you have in your hands. Your mission is too great to rely on these resources. You must get your eyes on a supernatural God and get plugged into His plan of abundant provision and continual supply. As long as you are doing God's work in God's way, you will never lack provision.

The cry of the world is the same as these sons of the prophets and the multitudes: "What shall we eat?"

You have the bread of life. Give it to them and let them eat and live.

CHAPTER TWENTY-ONE

HEALING LEPROSY

*N*ow Naaman, captain of the host of the king of Syria, was a great man with his master, and honourable, because by him the Lord had given deliverance unto Syria: he was also a mighty man in valour, but he was a leper. And the Syrians had gone out by companies, and had brought away captive out of the land of Israel a little maid; and she waited on Naaman's wife. And she said unto her mistress, Would God my Lord were with the prophet that is in Samaria! for he would recover him of his leprosy. And one went in, and told his lord, saying, Thus and thus said the maid that is of the land of Israel. And the king of Syria said, Go to, go, and I will send a letter unto the king of Israel. And he departed, and took with him ten talents of silver, and six thousand pieces of gold, and ten changes of raiment. And he brought the letter to the king of Israel, saying, Now when this letter is come unto thee, behold, I have therewith sent Naaman my servant to thee, that thou mayest recover him of his leprosy. And it came to pass, when the king of Israel had read the letter, that he rent his clothes, and said, Am I God, to kill and to make alive, that this man doth send unto me to recover a man of his leprosy? wherefore consider, I pray you, and see how he seeketh a quarrel against me. And it was so, when Elisha the man of God had heard that the king of Israel had rent his clothes, that he sent to the king, saying, Wherefore hast thou rent thy clothes? let him come now to me, and he shall know that there is a prophet in Israel. So Naaman came with his horses and with his chariot, and stood at the door of the house of Elisha. And Elisha sent a messenger unto him, saying, Go and wash in the Jordan seven times, and thy flesh shall come again to thee, and thou shalt be clean. But Naaman was wroth, and went away, and said, Behold, I thought, He will surely come out to me, and stand, and call on the name of the Lord his God, and strike his hand over the place, and recover the leper. Are not Abana and Pharpar, rivers of Damascus, better than all the waters of Israel? may I not wash in them, and be clean? So he turned and went away in a rage. And his servants came near, and spake unto him, and said, My father, if the prophet had bid thee do some great thing, wouldest thou not have done it? how much rather then, when he saith to thee, Wash, and be clean? Then went he down, and dipped himself seven times in Jordan, according to the saying of the man of God: and his flesh came again like unto the flesh of a little child, and he was clean. And he returned *to the man of God, he and all his company, and came, and stood before him: and he said, Behold, now I know that there is no God in all earth, but in Israel: now therefore, I pray thee, take a blessing of thy servant. But he said, As the Lord liveth, before whom I stand, I will receive none. And he urged him to take it; but he refused.*

2 Kings 5:1-16

In this chapter, we visit Syria, a heathen nation to the north of Israel. There we meet a man named Naaman, which comes from the Hebrew verb *"naem"* which means "delightful, pleasant, and beautiful." He was the captain of the army of the King of Aram, was a great man, and was highly respected. But he had a problem. He was a leper.

In Scripture, leprosy is a symbol of man's spiritual condition apart from God. Many today are perishing from the leprosy of sin. They may be wealthy, beautiful, and popular, but without God they are lepers spiritually.

The Greek word from which leprosy is derived means to "peel off in scales." Leprosy begins within and then erupts on the skin, gradually eating away body parts. Because it is highly contagious, lepers in Bible times were outcasts of society and wore garments identifying themselves as such. They lived outside of the city walls and were required to cry out "unclean" wherever they went in order to warn others. The pain of leprosy was not acute because it killed the nerves in the affected areas, but it kept the victim miserable, frustrated, and deformed.

What a classic picture of sin! Sin begins in the heart and manifests itself in the flesh. It gradually eats away at a soul that is numbed by the effects of evil. Sin's victims are miserable, frustrated, and deformed. Leprosy was incurable by man, just as sin is incurable by man. There is nothing man can do to deal with the sin that separates him from God, just as leprosy separated people from society in Bible times.

Naaman was a great man, but he had leprosy. Into this tragic scene enters a little, unnamed servant girl, insignificant to men, living under dire circumstances. One day she said to her mistress, *"...Would God my Lord were with the prophet that is in Samaria, for he would recover him of his leprosy"* (2 Kings 5:3).

Someone bore news of her comment to the king of Syria, who prepared gold, silver, and raiment to send to the King of Israel requesting help for Naaman:

And it came to pass, when the king of Israel had read the letter, that he rent his clothes, and said, Am I God, to kill and to make alive, that this man doth send unto me to recover a man of his leprosy? wherefore consider, I pray you, and see how he seeketh a quarrel against me. And it was so, when Elisha the man of God had heard that the king of Israel had rent his clothes, that he sent to the king, saying, Wherefore hast thou rent thy clothes? let him come now to me, and he shall know that there is a prophet in Israel.

2 Kings 5:7-8

When Naaman showed up, gifts in hand, the king of Israel was distraught because he knew he had no power to heal. The spirit and power of Elijah of which we are learning cannot be purchased.

LET HIM COME TO ME

When Elisha heard of the plight of the king and his distress, he said, "Let him come unto me..." Can you say that to those in need? Those have the Elijah anointing can!

So Naaman came with his horses and with his chariot, and stood at the door of the house of Elisha. And Elisha sent a messenger unto him, saying, Go and wash in the Jordan seven times, and thy flesh shall come again to thee, and thou shalt be clean. But Naaman was wroth, and went away, and said, Behold, I thought, He will surely come out to me, and stand, and call on the name of the Lord his God, and strike his hand over the place, and recover the leper. Are not Abana and Pharpar, rivers of Damascus, better than all the waters of Israel? may I not wash in them, and be clean? So he turned and went away in a rage.

2 Kings 5:9-12

Naaman condescended to go to the prophet's house, but Elisha didn't even come out to meet him. He simply sent orders for him to go wash in the Jordan River seven times, declaring that he would be healed. Naaman was furious. Not only had the prophet failed to meet with him personally, he had commanded him to wash in the muddy waters of Jordan. Why not the waters of Abana and Pharpar, rivers in Damascus which were better known and had cleaner waters?

Naaman's basic problem was pride and human reasoning. He said, "Behold I thought." He had a preconceived notion of how he should be healed. He wanted to be healed his way. How like sinful man!

Then Naaman's servant appealed to him saying,

> ...My father, if the prophet had bid thee do some great thing, wouldest thou not have done it? how much rather then, when he saith to thee, Wash, and be clean? Then went he down, and dipped himself seven times in Jordan, according to the saying of the man of God: and his flesh came again like unto the flesh of a little child, and he was clean.

> 2 Kings 5:13-14

If we are to receive miracles from God, we must put aside our pride and human reasoning. In obedience to the prophet, Naaman went to the Jordan River and immersed himself. Once, twice, three times, and on the seventh time, his flesh became like that of a child. He was totally healed! He was cleansed *"according to the saying of the man of God,"* just as we are cleansed according to the Word of the man of God, Christ Jesus.

Naaman immediately returned to the prophet to express his gratitude and said:

> Behold, now I know that there is no God in all earth, but in Israel: now therefore, I pray thee, take a blessing of thy servant. But he said, As the Lord liveth, before whom I stand, I will receive none. And he urged him to take it; but he refused.

> 2 Kings 5:15-16

Naaman offered Elisha a gift in return for his healing, but Elisha refused and Naaman departed.

A SAD FOOTNOTE

There is a sad footnote to this chapter. Gehazi, the servant of Elisha, decided he could profit from Naaman's miraculous healing:

> But Gehazi, the servant of Elisha the man of God, said, Behold, my master hath spared Naaman this Syrian, in not receiving at his hands that which he brought: but, as the Lord liveth, I will run after him, and take somewhat of him. So Gehazi followed after Naaman. And when Naaman saw him running after him, he lighted down from the chariot to meet him, and said, Is all well? And he said, All is well. My master hath sent me, saying, Behold, even now there be come to me

from mount Ephraim two young men of the sons of the prophets: give them, I pray thee, a talent of silver, and two changes of garments. And Naaman said, Be content, take two talents. And he urged him, and bound two talents of silver in two bags, with two changes of garments, and laid them upon two of his servants; and they bare them before him. And when he came to the tower, he took them from their hand, and bestowed them in the house: and he let the men go, and they departed. But he went in, and stood before his master. And Elisha said unto him, Whence comest thou, Gehazi? And he said, Thy servant went no whither. And he said unto him, Went not mine heart with thee, when the man turned again from his chariot to meet thee? Is it a time to receive money, and to receive garments, and oliveyards, and vineyards, and sheep, and oxen, and menservants, and maidservants? The leprosy therefore of Naaman shall cleave unto thee, and unto thy seed for ever. And he went out from his presence a leper as white as snow.

2 Kings 5:20-27

Gehazi was Elisha's servant, just as Elisha had served Elijah. He was also Elisha's student. Would Gehazi eventually have received the double-portion anointing as Elisha had? Would Elisha's powerful ministry have been bestowed upon him? We will never know because of this tragic failure.

When Gehazi decided he could profit from this miracle, he declared, *"As the Lord lives, I will run after him."* Elisha often used the phrase, *"As the Lord lives."* Gehazi tried to conceal his greed in the cloak of religion. He followed Naaman down the road, stopped the chariot, and asked for two talents of silver and two changes of garments. Naaman obliged, and Gehazi took these items home and hid them in his house.

When Gehazi appeared before Elisha, the Lord revealed what he had done. Elisha questioned where he had been, and Gehazi replied, "Thy servant went no where." Then Elisha sadly said:

...Went not mine heart with thee, when the man turned again from his chariot to meet thee? Is it a time to receive money, and to receive garments, and oliveyards, and vineyards, and sheep, and oxen, and menservants, and maidservants? The leprosy therefore of Naaman shall cleave unto thee, and unto thy seed for ever. And he went out from his presence a leper as white as snow.

2 Kings 5:26-27

As an Elijah, there will be those who you mentor who will turn out not to be Elisha quality. They will not be faithful men. Like Gehazi, they will have basic flaws in their character with which they refuse to deal. God will reveal this, and they will be subtracted from your number. God cannot use those who lie and deceive, neither can he use those whose hearts are set on profit.

Naaman's sin was pride. Gehazi's sin was greed. Both will destroy your ministry. Gehazi threw away so much for so little. Over the years of my ministry, I have seen many great leaders fall because of the appeal of pride, greed, and immorality. Don't let this happen to you. There is a similar account in the book of Acts, where Philip was preaching in Samaria:

> But there was a certain man, called Simon , which beforetime in the same city used sorcery, and bewitched the people of Samaria, giving out that himself was some great one: To whom they all gave heed, from the least to the greatest, saying, This man is the great power of God. And to him they had regard, because that of long time he had bewitched them with sorceries. But when they believed Philip preaching the things concerning the kingdom of God, and the name of Jesus Christ, they were baptized, both men and women. Then Simon himself believed also: and when he was baptized, he continued with Philip, and wondered, beholding the miracles and signs which were done. Now when the apostles which were at Jerusalem heard that Samaria had received the word of God, they sent unto them Peter and John: Who, when they were come down, prayed for them, that they might receive the Holy Ghost:(For as yet he was fallen upon none of them: only they were baptized in the name of the Lord Jesus.) Then laid they their hands on them, and they received the Holy Ghost. And when Simon saw that through laying on of the apostles' hands the Holy Ghost was given, he offered them money, Saying, Give me also this power, that on whomsoever I lay hands, he may receive the Holy Ghost. But Peter said unto him, Thy money perish with thee, because thou hast thought that the gift of God may be purchased with money. Thou hast neither part nor lot in this matter: for thy heart is not right in the sight of God. Repent therefore of this thy wickedness, and pray God, if perhaps the thought of thine heart may be forgiven thee. For I perceive that thou art in the gall of bitterness, and in the bond of iniquity. Then answered Simon , and said, Pray ye to the Lord for me, that none of these things which ye have spoken come upon me.

Acts 8:9-24

The Elijah anointing cannot be bought or sold. It cannot rest upon men and women whose lives don't line up with the Word of God. This ministry has no place for those who would make merchandise of it. Contentment is an important quality of those who would be used of God. Their hearts are focused on the Kingdom of God rather than possessions or power.

DO NOT FOCUS ON FAILURES

As you raise up men and women to walk in the spirit and power of Elijah, there will be those who return to the world, as Gehazi and as Paul's servant, Demas, did (2 Timothy 4:10). You may even have a Judas among your followers, as Jesus did.

Do not focus on those who fail; like Elisha, Paul, and Jesus, continue to focus on the mission: Mentoring men and women in the spirit and power of Elijah, preparing them for the double-portion anointing to flow through them to a hurting world.

CHAPTER TWENTY-TWO

THE SONS OF THE PROPHETS

*A*nd the sons of the prophets said unto Elisha, Behold now, the *place where we dwell with thee is too strait for us. Let us go, we pray thee, unto Jordan, and take thence every man a beam, and let us make us a place there, where we may dwell. And he answered, Go ye. And one said, Be content, I pray thee, and go with thy servants. And he answered, I will go. So he went with them. And when they came to Jordan, they cut down wood. But as one was felling a beam, the axe head fell into the water: and he cried, and said, Alas, master! for it was borrowed. And the man of God said, Where fell it? And he shewed him the place. And he cut down a stick, and cast it in thither; and the iron did swim. Therefore said he, Take it up to thee. And he put out his hand, and took it.*

2 Kings 6:1-7

We have encountered them several times. Who exactly were these sons of the prophets?

In contrast to the sad account of Gehazi in the last chapter, we find a whole school of men who were being mentored by Elisha who were devoted to the spread of the Word of God.

These men were apparently the ones who had followed Elijah and Elisha and stood afar off to witness the miraculous departure of Elijah. After Elisha used the mantle to roll back the waters of Jordan, the prophets came to him and said:

...The spirit of Elijah doth rest on Elisha. And they came to meet him, and bowed themselves to the ground before him.

2 Kings 2:15

From that time on, Elisha began to mentor these men. As we witnessed in 2 Kings 4, they were in session when the poisoned pot of stew was healed and God multiplied the bread and corn.

Elisha was faithfully preparing others to receive his mantle, and the number of students grew so large and they needed bigger accommodations. In this brief account, we see several qualities exhibited by these men which are important characteristics in those we choose to mentor.

They were problem-solvers. Instead of coming to Elisha only with the problem, they presented the problem and a possible solution. They explained the need for larger accommodations and presented a plan to solve the need.

They were submissive to Elisha. They asked his approval for their plan to build larger accommodations.

They were industrious. They didn't ask Elisha to hire laborers to do the work. Each one took personal responsibility for the task.

They proceeded with their vision despite limited resources. The fact that they had to borrow an axe for the construction project indicates that their resources were limited. Do not let resources prevent you from advancing the Kingdom. Start with what you have and believe God to meet the need.

They were honest and respectful of the property of others. The man who lost the borrowed axe head didn't try to cover it up. He admitted the loss and expressed distress over it. In that day, any kind of iron was scarce, so this was a tremendous loss. Character is what authenticates the message we bear to the world. It shows that the message has impacted the messenger. This is vital to the selection of those to whom you would pass on the mantle of the anointing. It is evident these sons of the prophets that Elisha was training were men of character.

CHARACTERISTICS OF ELISHAS

As you raise up Elishas under your ministry, there are several important characteristics they must possess in addition to those evidenced in the sons of the prophets.

Faithfulness: Paul told Timothy to select faithful people and commit to them the things he had been taught. These faithful people were to have the ability to teach others. The basic requirements are faithfulness and the ability to teach others. If a person is not faithful, he will not fulfill his responsibility of spiritual reproduction. If he is faithful but does not know how to teach others, then he will also fail. Faithfulness involves spiritual maturity, but faithful men are not necessarily faultless men. They are believers who are in the process of developing Christ-like qualities in their lives. Even faithful men have problems and weaknesses to overcome, as we learned in Elijah's incident of despondency. The world takes talented men and attempts to give them character. They focus on creating professionals. God said to take faithful men of character and He will empower them with spiritual talents and abilities. Both Elijah and Elisha were faithful to their God-given tasks.

Availability: Select men and women who are available. When Elijah threw his mantle on Elisha, he left all to follow. When Jesus selected Simon and Andrew, they immediately left their nets. The word "immediately" reveals their availability. Those you select must be available and willing to make this vision the priority of their lives.

Spiritual vision: Faithful men and women are motivated by spiritual vision. Both Elijah and Elisha could see into the spirit world. They were not limited to natural vision. When Jesus gave Peter and Andrew the spiritual vision of catching souls, it motivated them to leave their fishing nets.

Preeminence for the Word: Faithful men and women have a hunger for the Word of God, as did Christ's disciples. Their hearts burned within them as He shared the Scriptures (Luke 24:32, 45). The hallmark phrase of both Elijah and Elisha was, *"Thus saith the Lord"* as they delivered God's Word to the world.

Love for God: Faithful men and women are marked by a love for God and man. They take seriously the first and second greatest commands:

> *And thou shalt love the Lord thy God with all thy heart, and with all thy soul, and with all thy mind, and with all thy strength: this is the first commandment. And the second is like, namely this, Thou shalt love thy neighbor as thyself. There is none other commandment greater than these.*

> Mark 12:30-31

Elijah and Elisha demonstrated their love for people as they raised dead sons, provided food in times of famine, and responded to other needs of humanity.

A servant's heart: As Elisha, who humbly washed Elijah's hands, we must be willing to be servants because *"The disciple is not above His master, nor the servant above His lord"* (Matthew 10:25). Jesus said,

...whosoever will be great among you, let him be your minister: And whosoever will be chief among you, let him be your servant; Even as the Son of man came not to be ministered unto, but to minister, and to give His life a ransom for many.

Matthew 20:26-28

A GOOD MENTOR

This brief account of the sons of the prophets illustrates how a good mentor responds to need and uses every circumstance as a learning laboratory. Elisha didn't treat the loss of the axe head as trivial. He took it seriously and asked the young man to take him to the spot where it was lost. There, on the banks of the stream, Elisha threw in a stick and the axe head floated to the top. Elisha used every circumstance–even something as insignificant as a lost axe head–to demonstrate to his students the miracle-working power of God.

As you train Elishas, use every opportunity to teach them of God's supernatural power. Use your environment as a spiritual laboratory where they can learn to become participators instead of spectators in the things of God. That is what makes this The Elijah Institute a "school with a difference." No spectators.

A MESSAGE OF REDEMPTION

This story of the lost axe head is also a tremendous message of redemption. Mankind, like the axe head, is lost in the muddy waters of this world. Only by placing the wood–the cross–into the muddy depths of human lives can the lost be resurrected from the depths of sin; restored to their owner, the Father; and replaced into the hands of God to be useful again.

CHAPTER TWENTY-THREE

DEVELOPING SPIRITUAL VISION

Then the king of Syria warred against Israel, and took counsel with his servants, saying, In such and such a place shall be my camp. And the man of God sent unto the king of Israel, saying, Beware that thou pass not such a place; for thither the Syrians are come down. And the king of Israel sent to the place which the man of God told him and warned him of, and saved himself there, not once nor twice. Therefore the heart of the king of Syria was sore troubled for this thing; and he called his servants, and said unto them, Will ye not shew me which of us is for the king of Israel? And one of his servants said, None, my Lord, O king: but Elisha, the prophet that is in Israel, telleth the king of Israel the words that thou speakest in thy bedchamber. And he said, Go and spy where he is, that I may send and fetch him. And it was told him, saying, Behold, he is in Dothan. Therefore sent he thither horses, and chariots, and a great host: and they came by night, and compassed the city about. And when the servant of the man of God was risen early, and gone forth, behold, an host compassed the city both with horses and chariots. And his servant said unto him, Alas, my master! how shall we do? And he answered, Fear not: for they that be with us are more than they that be with them. And Elisha prayed, and said, Lord, I pray thee, open his eyes, that he may see. And the Lord opened the eyes of the young man; and he saw: and, behold, the mountain was full of horses and chariots of fire round about Elisha.

2 Kings 6:8-17

Because Elisha walked in the spirit and power of Elijah, God gave him advance information concerning the actions of the armies of the King of Aram, enemies of Israel. Everywhere the Arameans would go, God would reveal it to Elisha and he would warn the King of Israel.

This enraged the King of Aram and when he discovered it was Elisha who was warning Israel of their plans, he sent his armies to surround the city where Elisha lived. When Elisha's servant went out the next morning and saw the multitude of horses and chariots surrounding the city, he was fearful, and cried to Elisha, *"…Oh, my Lord, what shall we do"* (2 Kings 6:15).

The Prophet Elisha did not react to what he saw with his natural eyes, but to what he saw through spiritual vision. His eyes were not focused upon the surrounding chariots and horses of the enemy. He saw a greater army–the armies of heaven on horses and chariots of fire. Elisha did not see defeat; he saw victory! Elisha's servant was overwhelmed with fear because he was seeing only with his natural eyes.

Elisha saw something ordinary men could not see because God had given him spiritual vision to see into the supernatural realm of the Spirit. Elisha told his servant not to fear, that "Those with us are more than those with them" (2 Kings 2:16). Then Elisha prayed for God to open his servant's eyes. God heard Elisha's prayer and his servant was able to see that the mountains around them were lined with horses and chariots of fire.

YOU MUST HAVE SPIRITUAL VISION

To minister in the spirit and power of Elijah, you must have spiritual vision. You must be able to discern God's will for your life, your city, and your nation. God doesn't want you to minister according to what you see with your natural eyes, according to your understanding, or according to your circumstances. He doesn't want your eyes focused on your problems. He wants you to minister with spiritual vision focused upon His unlimited power and promises.

God wants you to pray with spiritual vision. In every circumstance you face, don't react according to what you see with your natural eyes. Pray according to what God reveals to you as His will. As you pray for your family, unsaved loved ones, your community, city, nation, and those you are mentoring, ask God to open your eyes and give you spiritual vision to see His purposes and plans. Ask Him to direct your prayers and anoint you so that you will pray and instruct your students according to what He has purposed.

THREE TYPES OF PEOPLE

This skirmish around Dothan also reveals the three types of individuals to whom you will relate as you minister. There are some, like Elisha, who see clearly into the realm of the spirit. They understand what is happening spiritually on this planet. These are tremendous men and women to mentor.

There are others, like Elisha's servant, who with a little help are able to see and understand spiritually. These people are open to the truths of God's Word and ready to learn. Draw them alongside, pour your vision into them, and take them to the next level in God.

But as in Dothan, there are many who are sleeping spiritually and cannot see into this higher dimension. They are content to live in the natural realm and do not want to be confronted with things beyond their natural senses. Until their eyes are open or they are willing to have their eyes open, they will remain oblivious to the end-time move of God.

GOD'S MIRACULOUS INTERVENTION

God miraculously intervened in this situation at Dothan and the Syrians no longer invaded the land of Israel:

And when they came down to him, Elisha prayed unto the Lord, and said, Smite this people, I pray thee, with blindness. And he smote them with blindness according to the word of Elisha. And Elisha said unto them, This is not the way, neither is this the city: follow me, and I will bring you to the man whom ye seek. But he led them to Samaria. And it came to pass, when they were come into Samaria, that Elisha said, Lord, open the eyes of these men, that they may see. And the Lord opened their eyes, and they saw; and, behold, they were in the midst of Samaria. And the king of Israel said unto Elisha, when he saw them, My father, shall I smite them? shall I smite them? And he answered, Thou shalt not smite them: wouldest thou smite those whom thou hast taken captive with thy sword and with thy bow? set bread and water before them, that they may eat and drink, and go to their master. And he prepared great provision for them: and when they had eaten and drunk, he sent them away, and they went to their master. So the bands of Syria came no more into the land of Israel.

2 Kings 6-18-23

Satan will not just sit back and let you go forth in the double-portion anointing. Like Elisha, you will be confronted with opposition. Whenever you face the enemy, ask God for spiritual insight and then battle according to the guidelines given by the Apostle Paul:

Put on the whole armour of God, that ye may be able to stand against the wiles of the devil. For we wrestle not against flesh and blood, but against principalities, against powers, against the rulers of the darkness of this world, against spiritual wickedness in high places. Wherefore take unto you the whole armour of God, that ye may be able to withstand in the evil day, and having done all, to stand. Stand therefore, having your loins girt about with truth, and having on the breastplate of righteousness; And your feet shod with the preparation of the gospel of peace; Above all, taking the shield of faith, wherewith ye shall be able to quench all the fiery darts of the wicked. And take the helmet of salvation, and the sword of the Spirit, which is the word of God: Praying always with all prayer and supplication in the Spirit, and watching thereunto with all perseverance and supplication for all saints.

Ephesians 6:11-18

SEEING WITH SPIRITUAL VISION

We are God's end-time prophetic generation! God is raising up a prophetic people who know the signs of the times; who are able to discern and know God's will in this end-time hour; and who are fully consecrated and committed to fulfilling His will before Christ's return. These people will be able to see with spiritual vision.

God intends for you to discern what He is doing. He not only wants you to know the prophetic season in which we are living, but He also wants you to walk in the prophetic fulfillment of His promises.

It is not necessary to have a master's degree in theology or biblical studies to understand the spirit world. These things are not understood through head knowledge, but they are discerned by the Spirit.

Through the indwelling of the Holy Spirit, you are able to have advance knowledge of what God is going to do, what He is saying, and to know the enemy's plans so that you can be prepared.

Under the old covenant, there was no "open vision," no revelation of God to man, and no divine communication except through the prophets. The Holy Spirit came upon the prophets and God spoke through them, but the Holy Spirit did not live within them.

With the outpouring of the Holy Spirit came a new day of revelation. The mantle of God's Spirit came upon the Church and the Third Person of the Trinity came to live and dwell within believers. Joel's prophecy is now being fulfilled. We are walking in the fulfillment of it as God's Spirit is being poured out in every nation:

> *And it shall come to pass afterward, that I will pour out my spirit upon all flesh; and your sons and your daughters shall prophesy, your old men shall dream dreams, your young men shall see visions: And also upon the servants and upon the handmaids in those days will I pour out my spirit.*

Joel 2:28-29

Today, when a believer is baptized with the Holy Spirit, the same power and anointing of the Holy Spirit that was upon Jesus comes to remain within them. It is not something that comes and goes. The anointing covers us like Elijah's mantle. It remains with us wherever we go. It releases God's power within us to fulfill His will. The Apostle John wrote:

> *But as for you, the anointing (the sacred appointment, the unction) which you received from Him, abides [permanently] in you; [so] then you have no need that anyone should instruct you. But just as his anointing teaches you concerning everything and is true and is no falsehood, so you must abide live in, never depart from Him just as (His anointing) has taught you [to do] [being rooted in Him, knit to Him].*

1 John 2:27 TAB

The anointing of the Holy Spirit remains within you. You no longer need to wonder what is going on around you because the Spirit living within you reveals it. Through the Holy Spirit, you are given spiritual vision to be able to see and hear things in the supernatural realm. Jesus said:

> *But when He, the Spirit of Truth (the truth-giving Spirit) comes, He will guide you into all Truth. (the whole, full truth.) For He will not speak His own message – [on His own authority]; but He will tell whatever He hears [from the Father; He will give the message that has been given to Him] and He will announce and declare to you the things that are to come - [that will happen in the future].*

John 16:13 TAB

YOU CAN RECEIVE DIRECTION YOURSELF

The major emphasis of today's prophetic ministry has been upon personal prophecy. Christians are running from one meeting to another hoping that they will receive a personal word of prophecy. God never intended the major focus of prophecy in this end-time hour to be upon personal prophecy.

Amos prophesied that a day would come when people would run from sea to sea seeking a word from the Lord.

Behold the days come, saith the Lord God, that I will send a famine in the land, not a famine of bread, nor a thirst for water, but of hearing the words of the Lord: And they shall wander from sea to sea, and from the north even to the east, ...they shall not find it.

Amos 8: 8-12

There are many who desperately want to know God's voice, to hear a "word from the Lord" concerning their lives and ministries. But, instead of waiting on God through prayer and fasting to receive His direction, they go to meeting after meeting seeking personal prophecy over their lives.

There may be times when God will use an anointed minister, teacher, or prophet to speak over your life, but the words they speak should be a confirmation of what God has already revealed to you. God has given you His Spirit and His anointing remains within you so that you can hear and know His voice for yourself.

Take a moment right now, bow your head, and ask God to give you spiritual vision. You will need it to accomplish the divine mandate God is giving you.

MORRIS CERULLO

CHAPTER TWENTY-FOUR

THE PROPHETIC MANTLE

In 2 Kings 6-9, we find the final episodes in Elisha's life, all of which illustrate the tremendous prophetic mantle under which this man functioned.

SAMARIA UNDER SIEGE

In 2 Kings 6:24-7:2, the city of Samaria is under seige by Syria, resulting in a great famine in Samaria. In order to survive, they were eating donkey's heads and bird dung! Some parents were even considering killing and eating their own children. Conditions were dire, and the King blamed Elisha (2 Kings 6:31).

In the midst of these dire circumstances, the Prophet Elisha gave a prophetic word:

> *Then Elisha said, Hear ye the word of the Lord; Thus saith the Lord, To morrow about this time shall a measure of fine flour be sold for a shekel, and two measures of barley for a shekel, in the gate of Samaria. Then a Lord on whose hand the king leaned answered the man of God, and said, Behold, if the Lord would make windows in heaven, might this thing be? And he said, Behold, thou shalt see it with thine eyes, but shalt not eat thereof.*

> 2 Kings 7:1-2

Chapter seven records the story of four starving lepers who decided to enter Syria and throw themselves to the mercy of the enemy. When they arrived at the city, they found it deserted

> *...For the Lord had made the host of the Syrians to hear a noise of chariots, and a noise of horses, even the noise of a great host: and they said one to another, Lo, the king of Israel hath hired against us the kings of the Hittites, and the kings of the Egyptians, to come upon us. Wherefore they arose and fled in the twilight, and left their tents, and their horses, and their asses, even the camp as it was, and fled for their life.*

> 2 Kings 7:6-7

The lepers came into the city and began to eat, drink, and take the spoils. Then, convicted by their consciences, they shared the good news with the king of Samaria. Thinking it was a trap, the Samaritans cautiously checked it out and found it to be true.

> And the people went out, and spoiled the tents of the Syrians. So a measure of fine flour was sold for a shekel, and two measures of barley for a shekel, according to the word of the Lord. And the king appointed the Lord on whose hand he leaned to have the charge of the gate: and the people trode upon him in the gate, and he died, as the man of God had said, who spake when the king came down to him. And it came to pass as the man of God had spoken to the king, saying, Two measures of barley for a shekel, and a measure of fine flour for a shekel, shall be to morrow about this time in the gate of Samaria: And that Lord answered the man of God, and said, Now, behold, if the Lord should make windows in heaven, might such a thing be? And he said, Behold, thou shalt see it with thine eyes, but shalt not eat thereof. And so it fell out unto him: for the people trode upon him in the gate, and he died.

2 Kings 7:16-20

Just as Elisha had prophesied, there was a discount sale on flour! Two measures of barley for a shekel and a measure of fine flour for a shekel–but the king did not eat of it because of his unbelief.

RESTITUTION OF THE SHUNAMMITE'S LAND

In 2 Kings 8, it records how Elisha warned the woman whose son he had restored to life to escape divine judgment of a famine:

> Then spake Elisha unto the woman, whose son he had restored to life, saying, Arise, and go thou and thine household, and sojourn wheresoever thou canst sojourn: for the Lord hath called for a famine; and it shall also come upon the land seven years. And the woman arose, and did after the saying of the man of God: and she went with her household, and sojourned in the land of the Philistines seven years.

2 Kings 8:1-2

When this woman returned after the seven years of famine, she sought to have her land restored:

And it came to pass at the seven years' end, that the woman returned out of the land of the Philistines: and she went forth to cry unto the king for her house and for her land. And the king talked with Gehazi the servant of the man of God, saying, Tell me, I pray thee, all the great things that Elisha hath done. And it came to pass, as he was telling the king how he had restored a dead body to life, that, behold, the woman, whose son he had restored to life, cried to the king for her house and for her land. And Gehazi said, My Lord, O king, this is the woman, and this is her son, whom Elisha restored to life. And when the king asked the woman, she told him. So the king appointed unto her a certain officer, saying, Restore all that was hers, and all the fruits of the field since the day that she left the land, even until now.

2 Kings 8:3-6

What a great illustration of God's providential care. The king was talking to Gehazi about the miracles Elisha had performed and Gehazi had just related the story of the dead boy raised to life—when in walks the boy's mother! All she lost was restored to her by the king.

If you have experienced great loss in your life, begin to believe God for restoration. His Word to you is: *"And I will restore to you the years that the locust hath eaten, the cankerworm, and the caterpiller, and the palmerworm..."* (Joel 2:25). God will set in motion providential circumstances to see that all you have lost will be restored so you will be able to fulfill your destiny.

THE TREASON OF HAZAEL

And Elisha came to Damascus; and Ben-hadad the king of Syria was sick; and it was told him, saying, The man of God is come hither. And the king said unto Hazael, Take a present in thine hand, and go, meet the man of God, and inquire of the Lord by him, saying, Shall I recover of this disease? So Hazael went to meet him, and took a present with him, even of every good thing of Damascus, forty camels' burden, and came and stood before him, and said, Thy son Ben-hadad king of Syria hath sent me to thee, saying, Shall I recover of this disease? And Elisha said unto him, Go, say unto him, Thou mayest certainly recover: howbeit the Lord hath shewed me that he shall surely die. And he settled his countenance stedfastly, until he was ashamed: and the man of God wept. And Hazael said, Why weepeth my Lord? And he answered, Because I know the evil that thou wilt do unto the children of Israel: their strong holds wilt

*thou set on fire, and their young men wilt thou slay with the sword,
and wilt dash their children, and rip up their women with child.
And Hazael said, But what, is thy servant a dog, that he should do
this great thing? And Elisha answered, The Lord hath shewed me
that thou shalt be king over Syria. So he departed from Elisha, and
came to his master; who said to him, What said Elisha to thee? And
he answered, He told me that thou shouldest surely recover. And it
came to pass on the morrow, that he took a thick cloth, and dipped
it in water, and spread it on his face, so that he died: and Hazael
reigned in his stead.*

2 Kings 8:7-15

Ben-hadad, the king of Syria was sick, and he sent his servant, Hazael,
to inquire of Elisha concerning his fate. Elisha told Hazael that the king
could certainly recover, but the Lord had revealed he would die at the hands
of Hazael. Elisha wept, because he foresaw the evil that would transpire
under this man's reign. Hazael, with carnal reasoning, didn't understand
what was happening. Why weep over a man who sought your life? He
didn't grasp the meaning of Elisha's sorrow.

Hazael returned to the king and told him that Elisha said he would
recover. Then the next day, Hazael took a thick cloth, dipped it in water,
and smothered King Ben-hadad.

JEHU ANOINTED KING

In 2 Kings 8, the historical account records the tumultuous reigns of
Jehoram and Ahaziah (16-29). Then in 2 Kings 9, a prophecy is fulfilled:

*And Elisha the prophet called one of the children of the prophets, and
said unto him, Gird up thy loins, and take this box of oil in thine
hand, and go to Ramoth-gilead: And when thou comest thither, look
out there Jehu the son of Jehoshaphat the son of Nimshi, and go in,
and make him arise up from among his brethren, and carry him to
an inner chamber; Then take the box of oil, and pour it on his head,
and say, Thus saith the Lord, I have anointed thee king over Israel.
Then open the door, and flee, and tarry not. So the young man, even
the young man the prophet, went to Ramoth-gilead. And when he
came, behold, the captains of the host were sitting; and he said, I
have an errand to thee, O captain. And Jehu said, Unto which of
all us? And he said, To thee, O captain. And he arose, and went into
the house; and he poured the oil on his head, and said unto him,
Thus saith the Lord God of Israel, I have anointed thee king over the*

people of the Lord, even over Israel. And thou shalt smite the house of Ahab thy master, that I may avenge the blood of my servants the prophets, and the blood of all the servants of the Lord, at the hand of Jezebel. For the whole house of Ahab shall perish: and I will cut off from Ahab him that pisseth against the wall, and him that is shut up and left in Israel: And I will make the house of Ahab like the house of Jeroboam the son of Nebat, and like the house of Baasha the son of Ahijah: And the dogs shall eat Jezebel in the portion of Jezreel, and there shall be none to bury her. And he opened the door, and fled.

2 Kings 9:1-10

In the remainder of the chapter, the word of the Lord is fulfilled just as Elisha prophesied (2 Kings 9:11-37). And as Elijah had prophesied:

Wherefore they came again, and told him. And he said, This is the word of the Lord, which he spake by his servant Elijah the Tishbite, saying, In the portion of Jezreel shall dogs eat the flesh of Jezebel: And the carcase of Jezebel shall be as dung upon the face of the field in the portion of Jezreel; so that they shall not say, This is Jezebel.

2 Kings 9:36-37

As you minister in the spirit and power of Elijah, every prophetic word from God that you speak will be fulfilled.

YOU ARE PROPHETIC SEED

The events recorded in this chapter all relate to the prophetic mantle that rested upon Elisha. Like Elijah and Elisha, you, too, are a prophetic seed. You are called and chosen by God to be living in these closing days of time. As this end time anointing is being released, God intends for you to bear a prophetic word to a lost an dying world. Jesus said:

Ye have not chosen me, but I have chosen you, and ordained you, that ye should go and bring forth fruit, and that your fruit should remain: that whatsoever ye shall ask of the Father in my name, he may give it you.

John 15:16

This is God's prophetic promise over your life. Through the anointing of the Holy Spirit, He has given you power to minister to the desperate needs of the world, heal the sick, and reach the lost with the message of salvation. Like Elijah and Elisha, this end-time generation has a divine prophetic purpose to fulfill.

Jesus revealed that one of the major end-time signs before His return is that the Gospel will be preached to every nation, tribe, tongue, and people. He said, *"And this Gospel of the kingdom, shall be preached in all the world for a witness unto all nations; and then shall the end come"* (Matthew 24:14).

As you go forth to minister in the spirit and power of Elijah, you will actually be part of ushering in the end-times and bringing Jesus back to earth. You are a prophetic seed. Begin to function under this divine mandate today.

CHAPTER TWENTY-FIVE

DEALING WITH ROOT CAUSES

Now Elisha was fallen sick of his sickness whereof he died. And Joash the king of Israel came down unto him, and wept over his face, and said, O my father, my father, the chariot of Israel, and the horsemen thereof. And Elisha said unto him, Take bow and arrows. And he took unto him bow and arrows. And he said to the king of Israel, Put thine hand upon the bow. And he put his hand upon it: and Elisha put his hands upon the king's hands. And he said, Open the window eastward. And he opened it. Then Elisha said, Shoot. And he shot. And he said, The arrow of the Lord's deliverance, and the arrow of deliverance from Syria: for thou shalt smite the Syrians in Aphek, till thou have consumed them. And he said, Take the arrows. And he took them. And he said unto the king of Israel, Smite upon the ground. And he smote thrice, and stayed. And the man of God was wroth with him, and said, Thou shouldest have smitten five or six times; then hadst thou smitten Syria till thou hadst consumed it: whereas now thou shalt smite Syria but thrice.

2 Kings 13:14-19

The Prophet Elisha was quite ill when Joash, the king of Israel, came to visit him. Old prophets never retire, so there on his death bed Elisha gave a powerful prophetic declaration to Joash. He told him to take a bow and arrows in his hand. The king obliged, and Elisha placed his hands over those of the king. He told Joash to open the window towards the east towards the enemy nation of Syria. Then he commanded, "Shoot!"

Then Elisha proclaimed, "...*The arrow of the Lord's deliverance, and the arrow of deliverance from Syria: for thou shalt smite the Syrians in Aphek, till thou have consumed them...*" (2 Kings 13:17).

Then Elisha commanded the king to take the arrows and strike them on the ground. Joash complied, hitting the ground three times and then stopping. Elisha was upset with him and declared, "...*Thou shouldest have smitten five or six times; then hadst thou smitten Syria till thou hadst consumed it: whereas now thou shalt smite Syria but thrice*" (2 Kings 13:14-19).

From this encounter, we learn several important truths that are vital to our mission to reach the world in the spirit and power of Elijah.

Win first in the secret chamber: What happened between Elisha and King Joash in the secret chamber that day determined the outcome of the battle with Syria. It is what happens in the secret chamber with the Lord that determines your victories in the actual battles of life.

Demonstrate your intention to fight: Elisha told King Joash, "Take up the bow and arrows." The Apostle Paul said, "Take the sword of the Spirit." By taking up your spiritual weapons, you are demonstrating your intention to fight.

Put your hands on the weapon: Elisha told the king to put his hands upon the bow, then Elisha laid his hands upon the king's hands. The strategy for victory is your hand upon the weapon of God's Word and His hand on yours.

Open the window: Israel's foe was to the east, so Elisha told the king to open the window eastward. God wants you to open up the "windows" of every area of your life to expose the failures, defeats, and bondages caused by the enemy. Open the windows towards the enemy and prepare to attack!

Shoot: Elisha told the king, "Shoot," and the king shot. The open window towards the enemy is not enough. The weapon in your hand is not sufficient. Even God's hand upon your hand will not win the battle. You must follow the command of the Lord of Hosts to "Shoot!" You must be proactive in spiritual warfare; not reactive. Execute preemptive strikes against the enemy.

Know the objective: Elisha told the king to take the arrows and strike them upon the ground as a symbol of his victory over Syria. The king did this, but only struck the ground three times and then stopped. Elisha told him that because he limited God by hitting the ground only three times, his military victory would be limited.

YOU MUST DEAL WITH ROOT CAUSES

The king did not really understand the objective of warfare. Elisha said the Lord wanted to totally consume the enemy (2 Kings 13:17). By striking the ground only three times, the king settled for only partial victory.

The Lord's objective for you is total victory in every area of your life and ministry. If you fail to understand this objective, then your victory will be limited. You must deal with root causes and continue to battle until the enemy is eliminated. The root cause is not drug addiction, it is what is behind the drug addiction. The root cause is not immorality, it is what fuels the immoral behavior. Always go to the root cause:

Looking diligently lest any man fail of the grace of God; lest any root of bitterness springing up trouble you, and thereby many be defiled.

Hebrews 12:15

If the root causes of problems aren't dealt with in the lives of men and women to whom you minister, then their problems will only continue to intensify.

When Israel invaded the promised land, God told them not to leave any of the enemy alive, but the Bible records that Joshua spared giants in three cities: Gaza, Ashdod, and Gath:

And at that time came Joshua, and cut off the Anakims from the mountains, from Hebron, from Debir, from Anab, and from all the mountains of Judah, and from all the mountains of Israel: Joshua destroyed them utterly with their cities. There was none of the Anakims left in the land of the children of Israel: only in Gaza, in Gath, and in Ashdod, there remained.

Joshua 11:21-22

Later on, the Bible relates that Samson got in trouble in Gaza (Judges 16); the ark of God's glory was lost in Ashdod (1 Samuel 15); and Goliath paralyzed the troops of Israel in Gath (1 Samuel 17). None of these events would have occurred, had not giants been left in the land.

Giants beget giants. Go to the root causes and deal with them. Don't settle for anything else that total, 100 percent victory.

CHAPTER TWENTY-SIX

BEING DEAD, YET HE SPEAKS

Now Elisha was fallen sick of his sickness whereof he died. And Elisha died, and they buried him... And the bands of the Moabites invaded the land at the coming in of the year. And it came to pass, as they were burying a man, that, behold, they spied a band of men; and they cast the man into the sepulchre of Elisha: and when the man was let down, and touched the bones of Elisha, he revived, and stood up on his feet.

2 Kings 13:14, 20-21

Elisha's ministry lasted at least 56 years, having begun as a servant of Elijah during the reign of Ahab and dying during Jehoash's reign, spanning the reigns of Joram, Jehu, and Jehoahaz. The recorded incidents we have studied are spread over half a century of ministry.

In 2 Kings 13:14, we are told that Elisha was sick with a terminal illness–the sickness whereof he would die. In John 11:4 Jesus said the sickness of Lazarus was not one unto death. The converse of this means that there is a sickness unto death. Divine healing does not achieve immortality any more than modern medicine does. Even those raised from the dead by Jesus eventually died, including Lazarus.

There are two types of death mentioned in the Bible. A premature death occurs when a person is turned over to the destruction of the flesh and dies prematurely so that the spirit might be saved (1 Corinthians 5:4-5). The second type of death mentioned in the Bible is appointed death and every man has an appointed time to die (Hebrews 9:2; Ecclesiastes 3:2).

In this brief passage in 2 Kings, we see that even Elisha, the great prophet of God who did many miracles of healing and ministered effectively in the spirit and power of his mentor, became sick with *"the sickness whereof he would die"* (2 Kings 13:14). It was his appointed time to die.

YOU WILL FULFILL YOUR DESTINY

According to the Bible, as an old man Moses had no effects of age–his natural strength was not abated, and his eyesight was not dim. Yet Joshua, another great man of God, was "old and well–stricken in age." God preserved one supernaturally, while the other experienced the results of natural aging. Their spirituality had nothing to do with it. Both were great, godly leaders. God will sustain you to fulfill your destiny whether you experience the natural processes of aging or you are supernaturally preserved.

We often make the mistake of living bound by the parameters of time instead of eternity. As a believer, you are already living in eternal life whether you live it on this or the other side of death. When a believer dies, it is the ultimate healing within the parameters of eternity. You will be healed by God, whether this side of death or the other side as you victoriously enter the presence of the Lord with a perfectly whole body, soul, and spirit.

ELISHA NEVER LOST THE FAITH

So, Elisha was sick, he died, and was buried. This does not mean he lost the faith or lost confidence in God's supernatural, healing power. He simply followed the way God has appointed until such time as the operations of this world are concluded.

How do we know Elisha never lost faith? Because there was more power in his bones than most of us who are living possess! Some time later, in the heat of a battle, the body of a Moabite was lowered into Elisha's grave. When his dead body came in contact with Elisha's bones, the man was resurrected.

One of the briefest recorded lives in the Bible is that of Abel, who was killed by his brother, Cain. The Bible declares of him, *"By faith Abel offered unto God a more excellent sacrifice than Cain, by which he obtained witness that he was righteous, God testifying of his gifts: and by it he being dead yet speaketh"* (Hebrews 11:4).

Like Abel, you can live so that your voice continues to be heard even after death. The double-portion anointing that you have received will not stop functioning just because you die. It will continue on as the Elishas you raise up fulfill the divine mission and minister in the same spirit and power that has been manifested in your life.

Being dead, you can yet speak through the lives of these faithful and anointed men and women.

EPILOGUE

THE MANTLE IS IN YOUR HANDS

In the closing pages of the Old Testament, God prophesied through Malachi that He would send a prophet who would go before Jesus to prepare the way for Him. *"Behold, I will send you Elijah the prophet before the coming of the great and dreadful day of the Lord"* (Malachi 4:5). A period of four hundred years–often referred to as the "silent years"– passed from the time of this last Old Testament book until the ushering in of a new era of revelation.

The pages of the New Testament open with the account of the birth of John the Baptist who was filled with the Holy Spirit while he was still in his mother's womb:

> *For he shall be great in the sight of the Lord, and shall drink neither wine nor strong drink; and he shall be filled with the Holy Ghost, even from his mother's womb. And many of the children of Israel shall he turn to the Lord their God. And he shall go before him in the spirit and power of Elias, to turn the hearts of the fathers to the children, and the disobedient to the wisdom of the just; to make ready a people prepared for the Lord.*

> Luke 1:15-17

John was to minister in the *"spirit and power of Elijah,"* which is our same commission today. What exactly does this mean?

PROPHETIC PURPOSES

We find a statement of God's purpose for John's ministry in the prophecy of his father, Zecharias:

> *And thou, child, shalt be called the prophet of the Highest: for thou shalt go before the face of the Lord to prepare his ways; To give knowledge of salvation unto his people by the remission of their sins, Through the tender mercy of our God; whereby the dayspring from*

*on high hath visited us, To give light to them that sit in darkness and
in the shadow of death, to guide our feet into the way of peace.*

Luke 1:76-79

Isaiah adds to this that John's prophetic voice was that of one: "

*That crieth in the wilderness, Prepare ye the way of the Lord, make
straight in the desert a highway for our God. Every valley shall be
exalted, and every mountain and hill shall be made low: and the
crooked shall be made straight, and the rough places plain: And the
glory of the Lord shall be revealed, and all flesh shall see it together:
for the Lord hath spoken it.*

Isaiah 40:3-5

John was given specific prophetic purposes to fulfill through his
ministry:

- To go before Jesus and prepare the way for Him.
- To preach repentance and salvation to those lost in the
  darkness of sin and turn many to the Lord.
- To proclaim the coming of the Messiah.
- To warn of coming judgment.
- To turn the disobedient to wisdom and guide their feet
  into the ways of peace.
- To make ready a people prepared for the Lord.

As men and women with the double-portion anointing, you–like John
the Baptist–will walk in this same spirit and power of Elijah. Your prophetic
purposes will be the same:

- To go before Jesus and prepare the way for Him.
- To preach repentance and salvation to those lost in the
  darkness of sin and turn many to the Lord.
- To proclaim the coming of the Messiah.
- To warn of coming judgment.
- To turn the disobedient to wisdom and guide their feet
  into the ways of peace.
- To make ready a people prepared for the Lord.

PREPARED BY GOD

As a young man, John separated himself by going out into the wilderness surrounding the Jordan River where he was prepared by God for his destiny. As we learned in the lives of Elijah and Elisha, there is always a time of seclusion where God prepares you for the work He has called you to do.

John was in the wilderness for about 10 years before God spoke to him that it was time to begin preaching.

> ...*the word of God came unto John, the son of Zacharius in the wilderness. And he came unto all the country about Jordan, preaching the baptism of repentance for the remission of sins.*
>
> Luke 3:2-3

POINTING MULTITUDES TO THE MESSIAH

John pointed the multitudes away from himself to the Messiah. He said concerning Christ, *"He must increase, but I must decrease"* (John 3:30). He was not concerned about drawing people to himself or his ministry, but only with pointing men and women to Christ. If you are ministering in the spirit and power of Elijah, you will not draw attention to yourself, but you will direct people to Christ.

My desire, as a man whom God has called as a prophet and apostle to the nations, is not to create a dependence upon me and the anointing that God has placed upon my life. I don't want people to look at Morris Cerullo and say, "What a wonderful man of God with an awesome anointing upon his life." During my entire ministry, I have always pointed people to God and preached that He will manifest the same miracle-working power through them that they see demonstrated in my life. My desire is that, through The Elijah Institute, a whole generation of Elishas will be raised up who will continue to function under this double-portion anointing.

You must point people away from yourself to God. The focus must be on Jesus. You—your plans and agendas—will decrease as His power and anointing increases in your life.

THE ANOINTING IS HERE

For years, I have prophesied that an unprecedented, awesome anointing is going to be released within the Body of Christ. This anointing is not simply coming on us. It will not just be felt in our midst. We will not have to work it up or pull it down. It will be like a river of living water flowing out from inside us. And now—that anointing is here!

As we look at the crises in the world today–wars, famine, economic and political upheaval–what is God saying to us? What is He directing us to do? God is saying, "Don't look back. Forget past failures. Forget lost opportunities. Do not allow yourself to become weary or fearful. Look ahead to the victories I have already established and provided for you! Focus your spiritual vision upon Me and My unlimited power."

The generation that entered the Promised Land was one that had been tried and tested in the wilderness, as we have. Their forefathers were unable to enter the Promised Land to take possession of their inheritance because of disobedience and unbelief, and they died in the wilderness: *"And to whom sware he that they should not enter into his rest, but to them that believed not? So we see that they could not enter in because of unbelief"* (Hebrews 3:18-19).

God wants you to take possession of all that He has promised and prepared for you in this end-time hour. He wants you to enter a new dimension of the double-portion anointing so that you can impact this world for the Kingdom and fulfill His plans and purposes.

An entire generation of God's chosen people failed to enter the Promised Land through fear and unbelief. We must be careful that we are not hindered in the same ways and fail to enter into this new powerful dimension where God's power is flowing through us to meet the desperate needs of the world.

If the Elijah generation fails to have God's perspective concerning its role in this end-time hour, if we do not move in to take the nations for the Kingdom of God, there is no hope for this world. If we fail to rise up in this hour with the Elijah anointing, there is no hope for the unsaved millions who are dying every day without God.

WE WILL KNOW NO LIMITS

John's ministry was limited to a specific time and season in God's plan. When God birthed the Church 2,000 years ago, He never intended it to know any limits. He breathed His *dunamis* power into the Church, giving us divine capability to preach the Gospel, heal the sick, cast out devils, and raise the dead. He has given us power, authority, and dominion through Christ over all the power of Satan and his demonic forces.

Jesus said, *"Behold, I give unto you power to tread on serpents and scorpions and over all the power of the enemy: and nothing shall by any means hurt you*" (Luke 10:19). Instead of being intimidated by the world and compromising the Word of God for fear of reprisal, we must take our position of authority to push back the powers of darkness in our cities, communities, and nations.

As Joshua and the new generation of Israel prepared to take possession of the Promised Land, God gave them dominion. He told Joshua, *"There shall not any man be able to stand before thee all the days of thy life: as I was with Moses, so I will be with thee. I will not fail thee, nor forsake thee"* (Joshua 1:5).

As Elijahs go forth to train Elishas and they train others, God is giving us the same authority. No one will be able to stand before us. As God was with Elijah and Elisha, so He will be with us. He will deliver us out of the hands of our enemies and healing and deliverance will flow through us to the world.

God told Joshua, *"Have not I commanded thee? Be strong and of a good courage; be not afraid, neither be thou dismayed: for the Lord they God is with thee whithersoever thou goest"* (Joshua 1:9). Knowing that God has placed His Spirit within you, then you never need to be afraid or dismayed. You can be strong and immovable. Regardless of the circumstances you face, you have nothing to fear.

AN ARMY OF ELIJAHS

You are a part of God's end-time plan, and you are not alone. You are part of a mighty army of Elijahs and Elishas that God is raising up around the globe. You are part of the end-time generation God is empowering to bring in the great final harvest of souls before Christ returns.

Jesus said:

But you shall receive power (ability, efficiency and might) when the Holy Spirit has come upon you, and you shall be My witnesses in Jerusalem and all Judea and Samaria and to the ends (the very bounds) of the earth.

Acts 1:8 TAB

The true ministry of the Church can be summed up in the words of Christ as He began His ministry on earth: Jesus said, *"The Spirit of the Lord is upon me, because he hath anointed me to preach the gospel to the poor; he hath sent me to heal the brokenhearted, to preach deliverance to the captives, and recovering of sight to the blind, to set at liberty them that are bruised, To preach the acceptable year of the Lord"* (Luke 4:18-19).

God intends the Church to be the healing center for the world and it is time for us to realign our priorities with His. He is not as concerned about our erecting great buildings and filling them with church members as He is about us reaching out to the poor, destitute, and lost humanity.

God is not as concerned about how many conferences, rallies, and seminars you conduct as He is about what you are doing to reach the lost. Jesus made it clear concerning His priority for ministry. He said, *"...for I am not come to call the righteous, but sinners to repentance"* (Matthew 9:13), and, *"For the Son of man is come to seek and to save that which was lost"* (Luke 19:10).

As Elijahs, we must have this same priority. Instead of spending 90 percent of our time and finances on ministering to church members and 10 percent on evangelism, we need to spend 90 percent of our time and finances on ministering to the lost and 10 percent on ministering to those sitting in our church pews.

It is time for the Church to get off the pews and out onto the streets, into the bars, prisons, and places where the need is the greatest. We must not allow our hearts to become hardened to the cries of the lost. We must have God's heartbeat.

THE HEARTBEAT OF GOD

When we began mobilization for our first *Mission To All The World* outreaches several years ago, God spoke to me and revealed His heart to me. I was in Brazil and had ministered to more than 60,000 believers in five days. The purpose of the meetings was to release the prophetic word of God over these nations and impart the *Mission To All The World* vision.

The Spirit of God spoke to me and said, "Son, tell My people what My heartbeat is."

> I said, "God, what is Your heartbeat?"
> God answered, "Souls...lost souls!"
> I said, "God, how can I tell people what Your heartbeat is?"
> He said, "Tell them I gave My Son for the lost."

You must have God's priorities and His heartbeat if you are going to rise up in the power, authority, and double-portion anointing of an Elijah Our focus must be SOULS! Jesus said, *"And the gospel of the Kingdom shall be preached in all the world for a witness unto all nations; and then shall the end come"* (Matthew 24:14).

The double-portion anointing God is pouring out is not just to make us feel good, or to inspire us to dance and rejoice. It is to enable us to get the job done! Don't look at the crises or the challenges you face in your city and nation and become overwhelmed thinking there is no possible way you will ever be able to minister to the desperate needs and reach the multitudes which are lost. Exercise the powerful anointing God is giving you through this mantle of divine authority. Do not focus on the overwhelming need; focus on the supernatural power of God flowing through you.

If you are facing strong opposition or persecution for the sake of the Gospel, you do not have to live in constant fear and defeat. See yourself through God's perspective. He has given you power, authority, and dominion. Just as God supernaturally manifested Himself on behalf of Elijah and Elisha, He will do the same for you. Do not retreat and do not back down. Go forward!

DO IT AGAIN, GOD!

In one of his Psalms, David declared:

> We have heard with our ears, O God, our fathers have told us, what work thou didst in their days, in the times of old. How thou didst drive out the heathen with thy hand, and plantedst them; how thou didst afflict the people, and cast them out. For they got not the land in possession by their own sword, neither did their own arm save them: but thy right hand, and thine arm, and the light of thy countenance, because thou hadst a favour unto them.

> Psalm 44:1-3

Then he cried out, *"Thou art my King, O God command deliverances for Jacob"* (Psalm 44:4).

In essence, David was saying, "All my life I have heard about what You did. I have heard about what happened in the past. I have told my children and grandchildren. We have been telling it repeatedly. We know what You did in the past, but You've got to do it again! I don't want to just hear or read about the miracles of the past. I want to be part of Your great miracles of deliverance in my day. Do it again, God!" That is our cry as modern-day Elijahs: "God, do it again!"

THE FUTURE IS IN YOUR HANDS

The future of this end-time work of God in the world does not rest in the hands of professional ministers. It is not in the building of churches or the launching of communication satellites. It is not in building denominations. It is not even by great preaching.

The future of the work of God rests in the hands of those who will pick up the mantle of the double-portion anointing and begin to manifest the proof-producing power of the Gospel that authenticates both the messenger and the message.

The task is great. There are more than six billion people in the world, and millions are added to this number each year. We are in a race against time. False religions are sweeping in the disillusioned of the world. We must take up the mantle of this anointing right now–today–and we must pass it on to the next generation.

The Church was not born through great orators or educators. It was born in the demonstration of power of which the Apostle Paul spoke of to the Corinthians where he declared:

> *And I, brethren, when I came to you, came not with excellency of speech or of wisdom, declaring unto you the testimony of God. For I determined not to know any thing among you, save Jesus Christ, and him crucified. And I was with you in weakness, and in fear, and in much trembling. And my speech and my preaching was not with enticing words of man's wisdom, but in demonstration of the Spirit and of power: That your faith should not stand in the wisdom of men, but in the power of God.*
>
> 1 Corinthians 2:1-5

This is the same mantle of Elijah, the same anointing, under which we must go forth.

We have traveled a long way together as we have followed in the footsteps of Elijah and his protégé Elisha. The mantle of this anointing is now passed on to you. Pick it up and begin to function in the spirit and power of Elijah. Use the double-portion anointing you have received, go forth in authority, and reach a lost and dying world.

APPENDICES

APPENDIX ONE

MIRACLES IN THE MINISTRY OF ELIJAH

- Causing the rain the cease for 3½ years
  (1 Kings 17:1)
- Being fed by the ravens (1 Kings 17:4)
- Miracle of the meal and oil (1 Kings 17:14)
- Resurrection of the widow's son (1 Kings 17:22)
- Calling fire from heaven on the altar (1 Kings 18:38)
- Causing it to rain (1 Kings 18:45)
- Prophecy that Ahab's sons would all be destroyed
  (1 Kings 21:22)
- Prophecy that Jezebel would be eaten by dogs
  (1 Kings 21:23)
- Prophecy that Ahaziah would die of his illness
  (2 Kings 1:4)
- Calling fire from heaven upon the soldiers
  (2 Kings 2:10-12)
- Parting the Jordan River (2 Kings 2:8)
- Prophecy that Elisha should have a double portion of
  his spirit (2 Kings 2:10)
- Being caught up to heaven in a whirlwind
  (2 Kings 2:11)

APPENDIX TWO

MIRACLES IN THE MINISTRY OF ELISHA

- Parting of the Jordan (2 Kings 2:14)
- Healing of the waters (2 Kings 2:21)
- Curse of the bears (2 Kings 2:24)
- Filling the valley with water (2 Kings 3:17)
- Deception of the Moabites with the ditches of water (2 Kings 3:22)
- Miracle of the vessels of oil (2 Kings 4:4)
- Prophecy that the Shunammite woman would have a son (2 Kings 4:16)
- Resurrection of the Shunammite's son (2 Kings 4:34)
- Healing of the stew (2 Kings 4:41)
- Miracle of the bread (2 Kings 4:43)
- Healing of Naaman (2 Kings 5:14)
- Perception of Gehazi's transgression (2 Kings 5:26)
- Cursing Gehazi with leprosy (2 Kings 5:27)
- Floating of the axe head (2 Kings 6:6)
- Prophecy of the Syrian battle plans (2 Kings 6:9)
- Vision of the chariots (2 Kings 6:17)
- Blinding the Syrian army (2 Kings 6:18)
- Restoring the sight of the Syrian army (2 Kings 6:20)
- Prophecy of the end of the great famine (2 Kings 7:1)
- Prophecy that the unbelieving nobleman would see, but not partake of, the abundance (2 Kings 7:2)
- Deception of the Syrians with the sound of chariots (2 Kings 7:6)
- Prophecy of the seven-year famine (2 Kings 8:1)
- Prophecy of Benhadad's untimely death (2 Kings 8:10)
- Prophecy of Hazael's cruelty to Israel (2 Kings 8:12)
- Prophecy that Jehu would smite the house of Ahab (2 Kings 9:7)
- Prophecy that Joash would smite the Syrians (2 Kings 13:17-19)
- Resurrection of the man touched by Elisha's bones (2 Kings 13:21)

APPENDIX THREE

A COMPARISON OF THE MINISTRIES OF ELIJAH AND ELISHA

Background: Elijah came from rustic Gilead beyond the Jordan River and was probably from a relatively poor home. Elisha came from Abel Meholah in Israel proper and appears to have had a wealthy upbringing (12 oxen would denote wealth).

Personality: Elijah seems to have been a man of moods and experienced great emotional swings between euphoria and depression. We see no evidence of this in Elisha.

Physical Appearance: Elijah was a hairy man (2 Kings 1:8), while Elisha probably was bald (2 Kings 2:23).

Ministries: Both were empowered by God as proof producers. As a result of the double-portion anointing, Elisha's ministry superseded Elijah's in certain ways:

- Elisha's ministry lasted about twice as long as Elijah's.

- The Bible records twice as many miracles by Elisha as by Elijah, evidence of the double-portion Elisha had requested.

- Most of Elijah's ministry was directly confronting powerful worldly figures (Ahab; Jezebel; Ahaziah). Elisha dealt mainly with common people–a widow, a laborer, a Shunnamite woman, etc.

- Most of Elijah's miracles were dramatic and judgmental, ie., the drought, fire falling from heaven, etc. Most of Elisha's miracles were deeds of compassion such as cleansing the waters of Jericho (2 Kings 2:19-22), increasing a widow's supply of oil, (2 Kings 4:1-7); cleansing a poisonous pot of food (2 Kings 4:38-41); feeding 100 hungry men by

multiplying a small amount of barley loaves and corn
(2 Kings 4:42-44); curing a Gentile of leprosy
(2 Kings 5:14); and recovering a lost axe head
(2 Kings 6:1-7).

- Both apparently trained the "sons of the prophets"
  during their ministries (2 Kings 2:3, 5, 7; 4:1, 38; 5:22).

- Both had unusual experiences in their departures
  from this life. Elijah was taken up without
  experiencing death (2 Kings 2), while Elisha's bones
  brought a corpse back to life (2 King 13).

APPENDIX FOUR

INDEX OF BIBLICAL REFERENCES

ELIJAH

The story of Elijah is recorded in Kings 17 -2 Kings 10:17. Elijah's name is specifically mentioned in the following references:

1 Kings 17:1,13,15-16,18, 22-24
1 Kings 18:1-2,7-8,11,14-16, 21-22,25,27,
     30-31,36,40-42,46
1 Kings 19:1-2,9,13,19-21
1 Kings 21:17,20,28,28
2 Kings 1:3-4,8,10,12,13,15,17
2 Kings 2:1-2,4.6,8-9,11,13-15
2 Kings 3:11
2 Kings 9:36
2 Kings 10:10,17

Elijah is also mentioned in the following references:

2 Chronicles 21:12
Ezra 10:21
Malachi 4:5

Elias, another name for Elijah, in mentioned in the follow KJV passages:

Matthew 11:14
Matthew 16:14
Matthew 17:3-4,10-12
Matthew 27:47,49
Mark 6:15
Mark 8:28
Mark 9:4-5; 11-13
Mark 15:35-36
Mark 15:36
Luke 1:17
Luke 4:25-26
Luke 9:8, 19, 30,33,54
John 1:21, 25

Romans 11:2
James 5:17

ELISHA

The story of Elisha is recorded in 1 Kings 19-2 Kings 13. Elisha's name is specifically mentioned in the following references:

1 Kings 19:16-19
2 Kings 2:1-5, 9, 12, 14-15,19,22
2 Kings 3:11, 13-14
2 Kings 4:1-2,8,17;32,38
2 Kings 5:8-10,20,25
2 Kings 6:1, 12, 17-21,31-32
2 Kings 7:1
2 Kings 8:1,4-5,7,10,13-14
2 Kings 9:1
2 Kings 13:14-17,20-21

APPENDIX FIVE

THE ELIJAH INSTITUTE

It was in 1962, in Puerto Alegre, Brazil, when God spoke to a young evangelist named Morris Cerullo and asked him what he wanted out of life. His response was, "Lord, I want to take the same proof-producing anointing that You have placed upon my life and transfer it to others."

Then God spoke to Morris Cerullo and gave him the commission that would shape his ministry, his life, his destiny, and that of multiplied thousands around the globe. God said, "Son, build Me an army."

In a world where national leaders were saying, "Yankee, go home", in an environment where missionaries were being expelled and missions closed, God revealed to Morris Cerullo that the key to a closing world was to raise up National Christian leaders to reach their own people. They had no visa problems. They could eat the food and drink the water. They did not have to spend valuable years learning the language and customs. Africans could reach Africans, Asians reach Asians, Latin Americans reach Latinos, etc.

God commissioned Dr. Cerullo to build an army—not a group of converts—but a spiritual army, trained to march into enemy territory and free captives from the bondages of sin, shame, and sickness. God revealed to him the key to a closing world was training national Christian leaders who could reach their own people with the Gospel.

"God showed me that to reach the world, I would have to raise up an army of spiritual warriors—not just preachers—but lay people who could be anointed and trained to go to their own villages, cities, nations, and people with the Gospel," explained Dr. Cerullo.

NATIONAL TRAINING INSTITUTES

Immediately, the focus of Morris Cerullo's meetings changed to training God's army, and he began conducting mass crusades combined with National Training Institutes around the world. Each evening, Dr. Cerullo would conduct powerful citywide crusades in which thousands were born again, healed, and delivered. In the mornings, he would sit with local Christian leaders and teach them the strategies that would release a similar proof-producing power and anointing in their own lives.

On the final night of the crusade, Dr. Cerullo would turn the service over to national Christian leaders who had been trained in the daytime sessions. One National would preach the message using the lessons learned through the transference of God's anointing. Another would give the altar call, inviting people to come forward and receive salvation, healing, and deliverance. Another would pray for the sick, the lost, and those with other needs. The arena would literally explode with excitement as the local leaders realized the power to work the works of God rested in their own hands, not just in the ministry of Morris Cerullo.

This on-the-job training prepared the National Christian leaders to return home and do the same thing in their own villages and cities. They realized the destiny of their nations rested in their own hands. Key leaders trained in these early National Training Institutes have spread around the globe and planted some of the greatest mega-churches in existence today. They continue to impact hundreds of thousands of lives for Jesus Christ.

THE EL CORTEZ SCHOOL OF MINISTRY

From that life-changing moment in that little Brazilian hotel room, Morris Cerullo has dedicated his life and ministry to building God's army and transferring the proof-producing anointing that is upon his life and ministry to others.

The next stage of the strategy which followed the National Training Institutes was the Morris Cerullo School of Ministry conducted at the beautiful El Cortez Center complex in San Diego, California. Dr. Cerullo sent trusted ministers out to the nations to interview and select national leaders who had been raised up during the National Training Institutes. Key leaders were selected to come to San Diego for intensive three to six months training sessions to further equip them to reach their nations.

The El Cortez Center complex included three motels, the main hotel, auditoriums, classrooms, kitchen, and cafeteria. For several months at a time, hundreds of Nationals lived, studied, and prayed together at the El Cortez Center as they went into the deeper revelations that are the hallmarks of Morris Cerullo's ministry–*the new anointing, proof-producers, spiritual warfare, and prayer.*

What made the School of Ministry a school with a difference was its emphasis on *heart knowledge* instead of *head knowledge* and on the demonstration of the power of God instead of passive learning. God empowered Morris Cerullo to transfer the same anointing that rested upon his life and ministry to the students. When these trained leaders returned to their nations, their ministries literally exploded as the new anointing flowed through them in salvation, healing, deliverance, and the prophetic.

After several years conducting the School of Ministry in San Diego, Brother Cerullo realized that he could never fulfill the vision because he could only get 1,000 people at a time into a session–and the waiting list multiplied. We were also leaving thousands of students at the borders of their nations who wanted to come to the school, but were unable to do so because of complications with visas and travel costs.

Of necessity, Morris Cerullo decided to take the School of Ministry to the nations. It was to become a "miracle campus unlimited," a school without walls.

TAKING THE SCHOOL OF MINISTRY TO THE WORLD

The commission has never changed. From the moment God gave Morris Cerullo the command to build God's army, that vision has remained the focus, although its manifestation and strategies have emerged in various forms.

The initial stage was the National Training Institutes. The second stage was the School of Ministry in San Diego. Then came the tremendous multiplication of stage three: The School of Ministry must go to the nations and become a school without walls.

Since 1983 when Morris Cerullo began taking the School of Ministry training around the world, he has literally crisscrossed the globe dozens of times conducting powerful training sessions and raising up a spiritual army that is impacting entire nations. Training sessions were conducted in existing churches, meeting halls, hotels, or arenas–wherever a facility could be secured.

An incredible multiplication began to occur at this stage. The School of Ministry sessions grew from 1,000 to 5,000, then 10,000, 15,000, to 25,000 or more. Tremendous men and women of God were raised up in these meetings who have built mega-churches and impacted entire nations.

This tremendous growth presented a new challenge: It was difficult to find meeting facilities large enough for the sessions and accommodations to house the leaders who came for training. For several years, Morris Cerullo sought God concerning whether he should build another School in a central location.

Then in the fall of 2005, as part of a vision that has come to be known as "The Big Coat," God revealed to Brother Cerullo the next step in the School of Ministry strategy. That revelation was The Elijah Institute.

THE ELIJAH INSTITUTE

The Elijah Institute takes key Nationals who have been trained through the School of Ministry over the years and equips them with resources, training, and anointing to raise up Elishas to reach their nations with the Gospel.

The biblical mandate is drawn from 1 Kings 19:15-19 where God instructed Elijah to transfer his anointing to Elisha: *"...So Elijah...found Elisha...and cast his mantle upon him"* (Portions of 1 Kings 19:19). The biblical strategy for passing on the mantle is the subject matter of the book you now hold in your hands.

The concept of the School of Ministry through the years has been focused on one thing: To raise up a new breed of ministers who can articulate and demonstrate the true meaning of the Gospel, which is *"...the power of God unto salvation..."* (Romans 1:16).

When Morris Cerullo accepted God's mandate to build Him an army, the cry of his heart was, "God, give me the ability to take what You have given me, the power and anointing that is upon my ministry and give it to others."

Since that day, this has been the driving vision, passion, and purpose of his life and ministry. God gave him his heart's desire to transfer the anointing to others. Just as the Prophet Elijah cast his mantle upon Elisha and a double-portion anointing came upon him, God has enabled Morris Cerullo to pass on the mantle of anointing on his life to spiritual sons and daughters of the Gospel who are now modern-day Elijahs.

The Elijah Institute equips these key leaders with mentoring materials and they raise up Elishas to reach the lost and proclaim the Gospel in a demonstration of the power of God, with signs following.

Armed with these materials, these Elijahs use The Elijah Institute as a stand-alone, short-term training program or add it to their existing schools and training program. The Elijah Institute, with multiplied thousands of Nationals worldwide–Elijahs who have received the training and anointing through Schools of Ministry, passing on the mantle to Elishas–will take the

School of Ministry to a powerful new level of ongoing multiplication!

- Elijahs mentoring and raising up Elishas...

- Elishas receiving the Mantle and producing more Elishas ...who then will go forth in a mighty demonstration of power to take their nations for the Kingdom of God and reap a great harvest of souls!

APPENDIX SIX

THE ELIJAH INSTITUTE MISSION STATEMENT

The mission of the Morris Cerullo World Evangelism Elijah Institute is to:

- Pass on the mantle of anointed, proof producing ministry from "Elijahs" to a generation of anointed "Elishas" who are committed to continue the cycle of spiritual reproduction.

- Equip key leaders—"Elijahs–to train those who have the spiritual hunger, capability, and willingness to be used by God as end-time laborers in the spiritual harvest fields of the world.

- Raise up men and women with the spiritual capabilities to be used by God in the supernatural, ordinary people who become extraordinary through the anointing of the Holy Spirit.

- Recruit a spiritual army whose members are capable of articulation of the Word of God and demonstration of the power of God.

- Raise a prayer covering over the entire world by passing on the prayer anointing and raising up powerful prayer leaders.

- Redefine the meaning of the word "minister" to include all born-again believers ministering in their spheres of influence.

- Demonstrate to the world the five-fold ministries outlined in Ephesians 4:11-13 for the perfecting of the saints, the work of the ministry, and the edifying of the Body of Christ.

- Establish a network of trained Elijahs and Elishas to overtake the lost in this generation and proclaim the Gospel to every nation.

APPENDIX SEVEN

THE ELIJAH INSTITUTE STRATEGY OF REPRODUCTION

The Gospel is to be preached to every nation. Can it be done in this generation? Only if the laity is trained to spread the Gospel message. When we speak of "laity" or "layperson" we are referring to men and women who are not professional ministers. They compose 99 percent of the Church population. This is the largely untapped potential that The Elijah Institute must reach and train if we are to fulfill the Great Commission.

Rather than separate the clergy (professional ministers) from the laity, we must help each born-again believer realize his personal responsibility in fulfilling the Great Commission. The world will never be reached with the Gospel if only the ministers are responsible for sharing the message. There are not enough professional ministers to get the job done. This is where The Elijah Institute fills such a vital purpose: Raising up key leaders who can train others to fulfill the divine mandate.

> *And he gave some, apostles; and some, prophets; and some, evangelists; and some, pastors and teachers; For the perfecting of the saints, for the work of the ministry, for the edifying of the body of Christ: Till we all come in the unity of the faith, and of the knowledge of the Son of God, unto a perfect man, unto the measure of the stature of the fulness of Christ.*
>
> Ephesians 4:11-13 KJV

THE EARLY CHURCH

Involvement of the laity was one of the keys to growth in the early Church. In Acts 8:1, we read that the persecution of Christians resulted in their scattering throughout Judaea and Samaria. Church leaders remained in Jerusalem and we find, *"...they that were scattered abroad went every where preaching the Word"* (Acts 8:4). Not only the leadership, but also the laity who were scattered fulfilled an important role in spreading the Gospel message.

From the beginning, the spread of the Gospel was a lay movement. Men like Peter and John were untrained fishermen. The majority of ministry and missionary activity in the early Church was accomplished by non-professionals, ordinary men and women involved in secular work as occupations.

When Saul tried to destroy the early Church, the Bible records that he entered into homes as well as the churches because he recognized that eliminating only the churches and professional ministers would not stop the spread of the Gospel. Each layperson was a reproducing Christian and each home was a center of prayer and evangelism (Acts 8:3).

WE CAN REACH THE WORLD IN THIS GENERATION

If we are to reach the world with the Gospel message and stop the advance of the enemy, the clergy and laity must join forces. Believers are not just fragments of the Church scattered throughout the community who come together for worship, instruction, and Christian fellowship. In daily work and living, they are representatives of the Kingdom of God who can reach people who will never enter a church or attend a religious meeting.

In the early Church, the spread of the Gospel was not left to the full-time pastors, prophets, evangelists, and teachers. Every New Testament believer was spiritually reproductive. If we are to reach the world with the Gospel, we must return to this strategy of the early Church. Both leaders and laymen must share the responsibility for spiritual reproduction. The growth in world population requires a return to the New Testament plan of ministry by each member of the Body of Christ. We cannot reach the world through token efforts and half-hearted dedication.

The command given by Jesus to believers is to "go" into all the world with the Gospel message. You do not have to wait for the command to go because it already has been given. In relation to the spread of the Gospel, the command is to go and watch for the stops, not stop and wait for the go.

TRAINING FAITHFUL MEN

Paul told Timothy to select faithful men and commit to them the things he had been taught. These faithful men were to have the ability to teach others. Through this organized plan of training the laity, the Gospel would spread throughout the world.

It is the selection of these faithful men and women that is the key to effective training of the laity. The world takes talented people and attempts to give them character. They focus on creating professionals. God said to take faithful men of character and He will empower them with talents and abilities to be spiritually effective.

By following the plan given in 2 Timothy 2:2, the Church can experience tremendous growth:

> *And the things that thou hast heard of me among many witnesses, the same commit thou to faithful men, who shall be able to teach others also.*
>
> 2 Timothy 2:2 KJV

Even on a one-to-one basis, the multiplication is amazing. Look at chart on the following page. This chart uses the period of a year as the average time necessary to train an Elisha and make him a reproductive, proof producing believer. In reality, the process could take more or less time, depending on the people involved.

But using a year as an average, if a National leader with the spirit of Elijah would reach just one Elisha and disciple them each year and have them pledge to disciple one person each year, the world could easily be reached with the Gospel message.

Observe on the chart that during the first year the Elijah is discipling one Elisha. At the end of that year, there are now two faithful men (Elijah and the Elisha he has trained). During the next year, each of them disciple one person. At the end of the second year, there is a total of four people, each of whom will disciple one person the following year.

WE ARE ASKING EACH ELIJAH TO DISCIPLE 12 PEOPLE EACH YEAR, HOWEVER, SO THE MULTIPLICATION WILL BE EVEN GREATER.

	ELIJAH(S)	ELISHA(S)		TOTAL
YEAR 17	65,536	65,536	=	131,072
YEAR 16	32,768	32,768	=	65,536
YEAR 15	16,384	16,384	=	32,768
YEAR 14	8,192	8,192	=	16,384
YEAR 13	4,096	4,096	=	8,192
YEAR 12	2,048	2,048	=	4,096
YEAR 11	1,024	1,024	=	2,048
YEAR 10	512	512	=	1,024
YEAR 9	256	256	=	512
YEAR 8	128	128	=	256
YEAR 7	64	64	=	128
YEAR 6	32	32	=	64
YEAR 5	16	16	=	32
YEAR 4	8	8	=	16
YEAR 3	4	4	=	8
YEAR 2	2	2	=	4
YEAR 1	1	1	=	2

Jesus entrusted the laity with the responsibility of spreading the Gospel. He took fishermen from their boats and made them into fishers of men. He believed that ordinary people could become extraordinary when empowered by the Holy Spirit. That is the vision of The Elijah Institute.

ABOUT THE MINISTRY OF MORRIS CERULLO

Dr. Morris Cerullo, President
Morris Cerullo World Evangelism

Morris Cerullo's accreditation for ministry is in itself quite formidable: a divine, supernatural call from God to preach and evangelize when he was only fifteen years old, and over half a century of experience as a pastor, teacher, author of more than 200 books, and worldwide evangelist.

Many honors have been bestowed on Morris Cerullo, including honorary doctorates of divinity and humanities, both by academic and spiritual leaders and heads of state around the world in recognition of his achievements and contributions to global evangelization.

Dr.Cerullo is respected and revered by millions around the world including over one and a half million Nationals trained Morris Cerullo's School's of Ministry. His major ministry outreaches include:

- **The Morris Cerullo Helpline Program** – a major television cable and satellite weekly hour long, prime time broadcast reaching out to hurting people in virtually every nation on earth.

- **The Elijah Institute and Schools of Ministry** – training national pastors, ministers and laypeople to reach their nations for Christ.

- **Mission to all the World** – reaching the entire world, region by region,with School of Ministry miracle crusades, television prime time specials, and local Schools of Ministry designed to cover every villiage, city and town.

Dr. Cerullo has made a tremendous impact on the destiny of the nations of the world. He has sacrificially dedicated his life to helping hurting people and to training others who will take the message God has given him and train others.

We Care